The Miracles That Follow

A Life of Meaning

SCOTT KRAMER

This book is dedicated to anyone who has carried the torch for a loved one. On a journey for meaning. To ensure their loved one's flame burns eternally.

Prologue

At some point in our lives, we will all become survivors. For some of us, that means that we will overcome a physical or emotional trauma to our own bodies. But for the rest of us, we will inevitably become survivors of a different nature. A less celebrated survivor. A survivor who survives someone who does not survive. Whether a friend, a mother, a father, a brother, a sister, a son, or a daughter, everyone reading this book at this moment will at some point survive someone near and dear to their heart. All too often the journey of this type of survivor is equally harrowing. Equally challenging. And equally heroic. This book is written for these special survivors.

My wife and I are walking this path of survival as we speak. A path that none of us ever envision. On January 4, 2018, we survived our then three-and-a-half-year-old daughter, Maddie. After her inspirational eight-month battle with a rare cancerous tumor in her spinal cord came to an end, Maddie's incredible journey was memorialized in our previous memoir, *Maddie's Miracles: A Book of Life*. As we promised at Maddie's funeral on January 7, 2018:

My commitment today, to all of you, is that Maddie's story, and Maddie's life, will not be remembered as a tragedy. But as an inspiration. I ask you all – as a way to honor Maddie – to join us in that commitment. It's okay to feel upset right now. It's a necessary part of the grieving process. But let us also see the light of inspiration through the clouds of sadness. That's what Maddie deserves. That's how to honor Maddie. That's how to support our family. And that's our collective path forward.

This book represents the fulfillment of that commitment. The story of the path forward. The story of survival. The story of preserving a legacy of inspiration. The story of finding hope in the darkest of experiences. The story of the miracles that follow. The story of a life of meaning.

PART ONE

The Search for Meaning (1/12/18)

A few minutes before Maddie passed on January 4, 2018, I stepped out of the hospital room. I had no reason to believe her passing would be imminent, so I walked over to the family lounge on the other side of the 16th Floor of Lurie's Place (our fictitious name for the Ann & Robert H. Lurie Children's Hospital of Chicago) to get a cup of water. The walk was just as much about clearing my mind as it was about having a drink.

Upon returning to the outside of Maddie's room, around 10:40 p.m., I saw her walking towards me. The same Emergency Room doctor who I had only seen on two previous occasions: on April 20, 2017, when she ordered Maddie's first Emergency Room MRI (cancer diagnosis day); and on December 18, 2017, when she ordered Maddie's second Emergency Room MRI (cancer recurrence day). Her name was Dr. Erin. We had never interacted other than these two (now three) occasions. On this night, however, she was coming up simply to say hello. To check in with us, after reviewing Maddie's records and learning that Maddie had been staying in the ICU and transitioning to palliative care. Surrounded by otherwise unfamiliar nurses and unfamiliar doctors on an unfamiliar ICU floor, I was comforted and touched by her arrival. I knew Pammy would be as well. So I headed into Maddie's room and gently woke Pammy from her sleep.

"Pammy," I whispered. "Dr. Erin is here. I thought you might want to say hello."

At that moment, Pammy lifted her head up from the bed, and she stared directly at Maddie's heart monitors. "Scott..." she trembled. I knew even before turning. As I looked up only to see previously life-filled lines go quiet. While meeting eyes yet again with Dr. Erin – for the third occasion in our lives – as she entered the room. Dr. Erin consoled Pammy and me, as the only familiar physician on this unfamiliar floor, right as the exact moment that we prayed would never come arrived in the quiet calm of the evening. With the shared embrace and tears of the only doctor who shared our darkest moments throughout this journey, Pammy and I again held each other as one in Dr. Erin's calming presence.

How can I explain this chance encounter? How can I explain the timing? How can I explain that Pammy and I had only seen Dr. Erin on three occasions: an ER visit yielding an MRI identifying Maddie's cancer diagnosis; an ER visit yielding an MRI identifying Maddie's cancer recurrence; and now an ICU visit at the moment at which Maddie's physical body was overtaken by cancer. The three lowest points of our life. With only one consoling, comforting, and common denominator.

I can't explain Dr. Erin's presence. But in the days that have passed since Maddie's passing, I have decided that I do not need to do so. Because, at this very moment, the objective reality of why Dr. Erin was present is of no consequence. Only the meaning that we choose to derive from our chance encounters will remain during our lifetime.

So why not choose a meaningful interpretation? Why not choose to believe in her protective presence or at least draw comfort from the moment?

Overall, the idea of choosing meaningful interpretations guided us through Maddie's battle. We found meaning in everything. In song lyrics. In Disney movies. In soup and two surprises. In "we'll see." In Daniel Tiger messages. In the developmental milestones of our younger daughter, Lily. In swimming classes. In dance moves.

We searched for meaning in the world, and we found life in the process.

Note that there is a difference between the question of whether things happen for a reason and whether we can derive meaning from our life's challenging experiences. At least in our brief time on this Earth, none of us will ever know definitively the answer to the question of whether things happen for a reason. But whether they do or they do not, we can continue to draw meaning from our life experiences. Small or large, predetermined or chance, there are daily miracles – or at least daily moments from which we can derive meaning – if we would only keep our eyes and ears open to interpret and apply them.

Pammy, Lily, and I now enter the vast unknown of life after death. Or in Maddie's case, life after life. As I look to a year of life ahead, I hope to be able to continue to find meaning and continue to live meaningfully. This meaning-filled mindset buoyed us throughout the first eight-plus months of our A.C. (After Cancer) lives, and I am confident that it will do so again. That's not to say the days, weeks, months, and years that follow will not bring challenges. They most certainly will. But by seeking and providing meaning in our daily experiences, we will continue to honor the most meaningful gift Maddie left behind: the gift of life.

The Seeds of Life (1/14/18)

In the darkest moments of Maddie's final days, I found comfort primarily in thoughts filled with life. For me, that meant two main mental activities: thinking about our vibrant and younger daughter, Lily; and thinking about how to keep Maddie alive even after her physical body would leave this physical planet.

As you can imagine, Lily alone ensured that we had a physical and parental purpose on this Earth. Since January 4th, I've told many family and friends some version of the following: "We don't have the luxury to break. We have to keep going. We have a job to do." This feeling of parental purpose was ever-present. And with each day that passes, I still cannot imagine what life without Maddie's daily smiles would be without Lily. But thankfully I don't have to imagine that unimaginable world. Instead, I just give thanks that Lily is here. Giving us purpose. Giving us giggles. And giving us life.

But even as Maddie's diagnosis grew darker with each passing December and January day, I was committed to creating ways to keep Maddie's light shining bright. And so whenever I felt soul-crushing emptiness begin excavating my heart, I replenished my ventricles with soulful plans. Plans of inspiration. Plans of hope. And plans of love. It was during these final days that I planted the seeds to keep Maddie's tree of life growing.

The first seed? Taking the blog form of *Maddie's Miracles* and putting the content into published, book form. The goal of this transformation would be to shine *Maddie's Miracles* (and the miracles and lights inside) upon other families who could benefit from its warming presence. From my perspective, childhood cancer has never been accessible from a public standpoint. Public awareness is limited largely to commercials that are more depressing than inspiring. More uncomfortable than beautiful. And certainly not relatable to those on the outside looking in.

Maddie broke down these barriers. She shined a playful and meaningful light upon childhood cancer that reminds us all of the sheer power of a child's innocent spirit. Maddie's approach to cancer not only offered guidance to other cancer patients and their families, but frankly, to anyone. Pammy and I began our journey thinking that we were teaching Maddie how to navigate life in the A.C. World. That we were writing The Narrative. But really, Maddie was the one teaching us all along. And through *Maddie's Miracles*, my hope is to share those teachings and shine her infectious and inspirational light.

The second seed? Forming a nonprofit organization in Maddie's honor. This seed spread quite quickly. No sooner did I begin to think about starting an organization than did I feel – with every bone in my body and every beat of my heart – the purpose behind this organization. To do what Maddie did best:

Bringing joy to the cancer experience.

As the light of this Maddie-driven purpose spread throughout my body, the name for the organization flashed before my eyes with equal exuberance:

Dancing While Cancering

After all, these three words epitomized Maddie's battle – or more appropriately, her dance – with cancer. For eight-and-a-half months, Maddie brought love and life to a place where many only see darkness and death. At this moment, I can still see Maddie – with multiple plastic tubes protruding from her central line delivering all sorts of toxic chemotherapy agents – dancing away on her self-made Lurie's Place dance floor to Coldplay's *Viva la Vida*. That image of Maddie literally *dancing while cancering* is the essence of Maddie. And I know, at this very moment – without any question in my mind – that our life's mission is now to share the same gift that Maddie gave us with the future Maddies of the world. To help other patients and parents approach the cancer challenge with the same beautiful inspiration and innocence as Maddie. I don't know where this dance will take us. But I'm confident that our cute choreographer will continue to guide our steps.

For now, the seeds have been planted. With a little more water, the growth process can begin.

Pancakes and Cheerios (1/15/18)

L eave it to Lily to continue to leave behind crumbs of meaning wherever she goes. This time it was breakfast crumbs. A little over a week ago. During the first meal that I experienced with Lily after returning home from our final Lurie's Place sleepover. Like any good PepsiCo family, Pammy and I typically offer some form of "good for you" option and some form of "fun for you" option during meals. PepsiCo's CEO often uses those phrases to describe their diversified food and beverage portfolio. On this particular morning, we poured a certain, healthy toasted oats cereal all over Lily's highchair tray. And in between, if you looked closely enough, you could find microwavable pancakes sprinkled in between.

When it comes to food, Lily cannot be fooled. I watched her closely over the course of the next fifteen minutes, and what did she do? Lily plucked out each individual pancake piece with surgical precision. The Princess of the Pincer Grasp pinched her way through the pancake portion of an otherwise balanced breakfast. In a raffle of not so fun food options, she found the pancake prizes that made her happy.

I'm officially following your lead, Lily Bug. These past couple of weeks, there are plenty of not so fun fish in my emotional sea. But I am committed to focusing on the symbolic pancake prizes on my life's plate. And that all starts with the precious face behind the mouth that was devouring those delicious silver dollar snacks.

Lily, you are the "good for you" and the "fun for you" option on our life's menu. Throughout life A.C., thanks to you, we never were able to fall too far. Because we had a job to do. No matter what life was throwing at Maddie, we owed it to you to bring 100% love and joy into our home. And lucky for us, you always made that effortless. Just as you effortlessly plucked your pancakes from the breakfast puzzle, we never had any difficulty finding your bubbly smiles amidst the A.C. challenges. We love you, Lily Bug. And we look forward to continuing to eat up the crumbs of meaning that you share with us as you grow older.

Miracle Update (1/16/18)

Today, I took my first step to water the seeds of inspiration we've been planting on Maddie's behalf: I met with an attorney. [Insert sarcastic lawyer joke]. As a novice to the idea-creation world, I wanted to make sure that we took the necessary steps to protect our rights and vet any legal issues relating to *Maddie's Miracles* and Dancing While Cancering.

With limited free time to explore, I met with an attorney who was recommended by a friend of mine. I knew nothing about her personally or professionally. Our first casual meeting took place over breakfast in a small coffee shop in downtown Chicago. As I introduced myself to this otherwise unfamiliar attorney for the first time, I couldn't help but notice her wristwatch. With an unmistakable, familiar face filling the face of the watch. The face smiling back at me as brightly as Maddie. The image? None other than Minnie Mouse.

I don't say anything. But then a few more minutes into the conversation, the attorney takes out the case for her eyeglasses. Who appears across the case? Why hello there, Mickey.

At this point, I can't ignore our seemingly fateful Disney connection any further. I learn that the attorney's one obsession in life is Disney. Her office is covered in all trinkets Disney. Her annual family vacations, one of which she leaves for tomorrow, take place in Disney. For anyone not familiar with Maddie's story, suffice it to say she loved Disney. And Disney, as well as its music, movies, and endless characters, played an instrumental role in Maddie's journey. So at this point in my chance meeting, I'm beginning to feel like I'm on a reality show where someone jumps out from behind a nearby wall and announces an earth-shattering surprise.

But no, the meeting was real. The attorney was real. Her love for Disney was real. And as with most miraculous moments along this journey, I can't explain the surreal coincidence. But I undoubtedly will draw meaning. And for this moment, I say it seems like a perfect way to begin our next step in this inspirational dance.

A Chair is Still a Chair (1/17/18)

I still remember the first time I returned to our home after Maddie's April 2017 diagnosis. As I reflected in *Maddie's Miracles*, I can picture making my way upstairs. In hopes of just taking a shower after who knows how many sleepless nights and showerless days. Making my way to the master bathroom, I had to walk past Maddie's bedroom. Only I couldn't do it. At the precise moment that B.C. became A.C., her precious, pink room was just a piercing and poignant picture of what life was just a few weeks earlier. As if walking past her room were like crossing the space-time continuum from our then A.C. reality into a B.C. life that I feared would never return.

Fast forward to January 5, 2018. Pammy and I returned home from Lurie's Place together after the final sleepover. I felt a grave sense of unknown as to my comfort with and reaction to returning home. Until the moment I walked through the doors, I wouldn't know how my body and mind would respond. From the toddler-geared books in our living room upon entry. To the characters and toy houses scattered across our playroom. To her precious, pink room. To her rocking chair. To the Maddie-centric toddler TV shows designated as favorites on our Netflix and Amazon accounts. To the pictures of Maddie, from birth until present, lining our walls and shelves. To her plates, cups, forks, and spoons. To our goodnight songs. To our memories.

To my surprise, Maddie's mementos wrapped their warm arms around me from the moment we met eyes again. Maddie is still here. We're still with Maddie. Unlike April, I now draw calm and serenity from the pieces of her life that remain. Even my night time routine is still intact. There are only small adjustments. After Lily goes to bed, I slip into the quiet of Maddie's room. I turn off her light. I sink into the soft rocking chair. I sing the *Shema*. And I meditate and reflect on Maddie's hope and inspiration. Occasionally, I break nighttime character by sharing some happy stories from the day now behind me or dreams for the day ahead. I say good night. And I close the door behind me before returning to our bedroom.

Before you conjure up an image of a crazy, bereaved guy staring at a wall and talking gibberish to himself, let's pause. Because I promise you, every bit of the experience of channeling Maddie is conscious, knowing, and beautiful. She remains my source of inspiration. She remains alive to me albeit in a different way. And I feel so blessed for the daily reminders scattered across our home. Leaving behind familiar and warming rays of sunshine.

Daddy, Come Get Me Revisited (1/19/18)

As you may recall, I used to begin my day with the sweetest sound in the world. The whispered words coming through the baby monitor.

"Daaaaaaaddddddy, coooooooooome geeeeeeet me."

At that moment, all of my morning mental musings muted. And I brought myself back to the present. To Maddie. To blessed joy. As I made my way into her room for the first time. Maddie willing me to feel gratitude for being alive.

Life today is no different. Just as Maddie's material world brings me comfort, Maddie's morning, meditative inspiration has not abandoned me. When I first wake, I take a few minutes of mindfulness to begin my day. I pause. I breathe slowly. I stretch my arms and legs. And while doing so, I channel Maddie's voice in my head, "Daaaaaaaddddddy, coooooooooome geeeeeeet me."

Although I know Maddie's physical being does not await me on the other side, her miraculous motivation never stops. In channeling these words, I'm channeling my desire to seek Maddie in a different way. To live in a way that brings me closer to Maddie's incredible spirit. To come get

Maddie through my words. To come get Maddie through my actions. To come get Maddie through my interactions. To come get Maddie through my plans for charitable change.

"Daaaaaaaddddddy, coooooooooome geeeeeet me," is now my morning meditative moment to bring my own inner Maddie to each day. And to continue my journey to ensure that Maddie's memory is an inspiration and not a tragedy.

With my morning meditation behind me, Pammy and I journeyed over to Lurie's Place on January 19, 2018. Bearing a laundry basket of *Frozen* and *Peppa Pig* toys, we headed up to the 17th Floor Playroom. Lurie's Place remains our home away from home. The place where Maddie's miracles and *Maddie's Miracles* began. And what better way to continue to memorialize those miracles than to spread Maddie's heartwarming joy to the other little heroes roaming the hallways. While we hopefully do not have any more Lurie's Place sleepovers on our life's agenda, our commitment to make the sleepovers more enjoyable for future Lurie's Place legends is only just beginning.

As we leave those toys behind…as we exit the 17th Floor doors…as we make our way down the elevator. Into our car. Cruising down Lake Shore Drive with the cold, whipping Chicago wind rocking our car. I hear Maddie's whisper. "Daaaaaaaddddddy, coooooooooome geeeeeet me."

We're coming, kiddo. One beautiful act of love at a time.

Seeking Sanctuary (1/20/18)

The Friday after Maddie's funeral, I stepped into the Temple Sholom sanctuary that faces east towards Lake Michigan just across from Lake Shore Drive. The main sanctuary is a sight to be seen. Whether you believe in God or not, and irrespective of your religious persuasion, walking into this one-hundred-fifty-year-old, handcrafted, awe-inspiring sanctuary, you feel confident that – if there were a God – the Almighty would be proud of this magnificent house of prayer.

After the inspirational, gratitude-graced experience of Maddie's funeral, Temple Sholom is very much a sanctuary for me. A sanctuary of respite. A sanctuary of calm. A sanctuary of meditation. A sanctuary of Maddie. As I sit in the seats where our family, friends, and community stood by our side to honor Maddie's memory, I cannot help but feel Maddie's presence. It's the last place we saw her physical body. The traditional moment of her memorialization. And thus a serene space to channel her living and beautiful spirit.

There is a difference between religion and spirituality that I never appreciated until now. Too often religious discussions or debates devolve into the tenets of the religions themselves: Does God exist? Which God is the almighty God? Is God omnipresent? Is God omnipotent? Is God to blame for our toils? Is God to thank for our spoils?

In the weeks that followed Maddie's passing, these underlying tenets and questions were of no significance to me. Instead, I found an equally meaningful secular and spiritual home in the Temple Sholom sanctuary. A quiet, beautiful space to channel Maddie. To meditate on Maddie. And to take a brief exodus from the noise of everyday life.

Enter Shabbat. From Friday sundown to Saturday sundown. For those unfamiliar, from a religious perspective, Shabbat is the Jewish "day of rest." Sure, there are religious traditions that many undertake on Shabbat – saying prayers over candles, saying prayers over wine, and saying prayers over a braided bread known as *challah*. But the secular, spiritual application holds the meaning. The concept is this: after a busy, stressful work week, we put down our labor. We put down our phones. We put down our busy minds. And we enter a sanctuary, both literally and figuratively.

Since Maddie's passing, Pammy and I have entered our mental and physical sanctuary every Friday evening. And in doing so, we receive the gift of being in what – to us – is both a house of prayer and a house of Maddie. A house of religion and a house of meditation. A house of God and a house of calm. As I type away this Saturday morning on my computer (certainly a violation of the pure, religious rules of Shabbat), I still can't answer many of the hotly contested religious questions above. But that does not change the value of spirituality in my current state of mind. To me, religion aside, we can all find sanctuary in a sanctuary. We just need to know where to look depending on what it is we're seeking at that moment.

Shabbat Shalom.

Miracle Update (1/22/18)

With the seeds of our Foundation tree planted, Pammy and I both know we have quite a massive forest of love to build. This will take time, dedication, and care. But in the meantime, we are still feeling so full of purpose and passion to give back. And waiting for the formation of the Foundation does not feel like a viable option. We want to do something sooner. To bring more of Maddie's joy to Lurie's Place before a fully functioning *Dancing While Cancering* begins. It was just a matter of what the idea would be, and where the inspiration would come from.

Enter our Lily babyproofing project. With a deep breath, and all too many tears, we began re-organizing our playroom at home. To store away Maddie's various toys and games and make room for Lily-friendly options (and frankly, choking-hazard-free options). Halfway through the reorganization, we made our way to Maddie's cast of plastic figure characters. What started, B.C., as a few Disney characters in a small bin slowly grew over the course of her treatment to literally 30 or so individualized plastic bags, each separately organized with its own "family" of animated figurines. Our own Ziploc condo of characters. You know the roster at this point: Doc McStuffins, Peppa Pig, Daniel

Tiger, Mickey Mouse, Hey Duggee, Bubble Guppies, Dora the Explorer…if there were an animated character, Maddie would have a separate home (or plastic bag) for its safekeeping. More importantly, these colorful characters spent more time with Maddie during her journey than probably any individual family member or friend. Maddie and her characters were inseparable. And the imaginative play they inspired could take place anywhere – home, a hospital bed, or an MRI waiting room.

And so as we removed these characters from Maddie's playroom closet, we knew another closet was calling. A closet in the 17th Floor Playroom of Lurie's Place. A closet that we will call "Maddie's Character Closet" and that will house individualized containers of figurine families (we'll spare Lurie's Place the plastic bag housing and class it up with some real containers). With characters aplenty, our vision is for existing and future patients to find the same joy and friendship that imaginative play with this cast of characters brings. And in a very poignant and Maddie way, we can shine Maddie's light across the 17th Floor.

Our purpose is calling. Our meaning is clear. One minor detail, we still have to get permission from Lurie's Place. But in the meantime, we'll be getting our characters ready for the big move we hope is coming soon!

Miracle Update (1/23/18)

We received confirmation today that the name *Dancing While Cancering* is currently available for legal use. Pending our attorney's search, we did not know whether anyone else was utilizing this name for their charity or business. But that search is over. The name is as unique as its three-year-old inspiration. We are therefore in the process of filing an "intent to use" application with the United States Patent and Trademark Office to protect our rights to have exclusive use of this Maddie-inspired name. While we have many decisions to make as to what this charitable dance will look like, we at least know that we have a legal name to symbolize the ideas to come. Until then, our dance continues.

A Map of Meaning (1/28/18)

Lily is starting to learn the difference between questions and statements. Whenever she hears an inquisitive tone in your voice, her response is the same:

"Yah!"

Never mind the fact that she has no idea what you're saying 90% of the time. She just gets a kick out of providing a positive response. It tickles her. You could ask her fifteen questions in a row. The answer will always be the same: "Yah!" I have to admit, her accepting, affirmative response brings a smile to my face every time.

I can also identify with forward-thinking instincts these days. As you can imagine, the most popular question that I field lately is some derivative of "How are you feeling?" Although my answer may vary each time depending on the questioner, generally speaking, I can honestly say that I am feeling as fine and strong as anyone possibly could in our situation. Pammy and I are both able to undertake our normal, daily functions. We're taking care of ourselves. We're eating. We're sleeping. We're working. We're spending meaningful time with Lily. We're visiting Lurie's

Place to give back. We're incorporating spirituality into our lives. We're keeping Maddie as a driving force in our lives. Overall, we're doing exactly what we set out to do – to continue to live with Maddie by our side. As an inspiration and not a tragedy.

That said, in the recesses of my mind, I can imagine other responses to "How are you feeling?" I can envision the concept of total breakdown. I can grasp the idea of losing faith in life. In God. In Purpose. I can see the role of victim. I can hear the voice of a more tragic narrator. Although these alternate paths are available, thankfully none have ever called to me beyond a whisper.

Oddly, while grateful for my response, I do not take a ton of self-credit for refusing to answer these more sorrow-filled solicitations. I am even reluctant to conclude that I am making a "choice" in my mindset. Because almost as instinctively as Lily responds with a positive "Yah!" to any question thrown her way, my natural approach to the A.C. challenge has always been to meet the pain with a heavy dose of meaning and forward-thinking. My mind and body refuse any other alternative. Because I know that the other choice, the darker voice, is not a real choice at all. It's an obstruction. A roadblock. An endpoint. It's not a viable path forward.

Although I am aware of this "choice," the gravitational pull forward contains somewhat of an uncontrollable, self-preservation feel. Interestingly, in my day job as a family law attorney, I am not trained to look on the bright side. I have had years of preparing people for their worst-case scenario. Of advising clients on what pitfalls await them in the face of various choices. Of conversing about the most painful moments of their lives and empathizing with them through their darkness. And yet when faced with my own perilous choice, I have never spent more than a passing minute considering worst case scenarios or pitfalls. I have instead squeezed every drop of meaning, love, and hope from this cancer lemon. I am holding on to lingering sweetness even though wincing in perpetual sourness would be equally plausible.

Altogether, this personal response – that is largely 180 degrees from my professional makeup – tells me that Pammy and I were made to move forward. We were built to last. We have the capability to survive in the face of soul-crushing sorrow. In doing so, we instinctively accept, for better or worse, each wind of the road with an implicit Lily-like "Yah!" Knowing that continuing to follow a map of meaning gives us the proper path to keep navigating this journey.

PART TWO

A Whole New World (2/4/18)

Yesterday was World Cancer Day. Ten months after our world was flipped upside down. One month after our world grew quieter. Although we could never have imagined our world looking this way, Pammy and I are still standing firmly in this world. Still well aware of the other-worldly strength and inspiration we witnessed. Still in awe of the world that Maddie left much improved.

As World Cancer Day comes and goes, Pammy and I continue our return to the world we once knew. Re-engaging our work world. Re-immersing in Lily's world. Re-exploring our social world (as this weekend we received a special visit from our dear friend, Ken, who literally lives on the other side of the world in New Zealand).

We do so, however, with Maddie still fully and beautifully a part of our world. Since January 4th, we've returned to Lurie's Place multiple times to give back to the 17th Floor world Maddie loved so much. Since January 4th, we've stepped back into the Temple Sholom world on multiple occasions to channel the strength and serenity we derive from Maddie's incredible preschool world. Since January 4th, we've gently journeyed through the various Maddie mementos in our day-to-day world: the songs, the pictures, the YouTube videos, the toys, and the many mental memories. An endless world of memories. Memories that give us comfort while also propelling us forward in this new world.

With Maddie memories filling our minds, Pammy and I will make our way to Dallas, Texas tonight for the American Cancer Society's annual volunteer event. A celebration of inspiration brought to us by one of the world's foremost leaders in the war against cancer. The same Society whose mission seeks a world with more birthdays. A world free of cancer. The event figures to be a fitting way to continue our flow forward into the world where Maddie motivates albeit from a different vantage point.

However forward-looking this event might be, Maddie flashbacks remain my fuel. As I went to sleep last night, I couldn't help but take another tour of Maddie's world. Dabble in the endless minutes of video clips. Hoping to again be a part of her world.

No sooner did I dabble than did I discover part of that world. Literally. As I spotted a video clip of a twenty-two-month-old Maddie reciting a good portion of her mermaid moment – *Part of Your World* – by memory. The clip says it all. Standing on top of a dining room table, Maddie might as well have been standing on top of the world. Because that's the space she continues to occupy for us – on this World Cancer Day and beyond – as we continue to make a mark on our world with Maddie top of mind.

We're also sending lots of love and gratitude out to the growing world of Team Maddie. In addition to the seemingly endless and soul-warming flow of cards, notes, and messages, we have collectively raised tens of thousands of dollars for various cancer charities. As of yesterday, the total donations to the brain tumor group at Lurie's Place alone exceeded $22,000. That does not include the additional funds flowing to the American Cancer Society,

The Anthony Rizzo Family Foundation, Bear Necessities, and a number of other incredible organizations.

Thanks to you, we continue to ensure that Maddie does what she does best. Being Maddie. And making this world a brighter place.

People of Action (2/7/18)

Team Maddie,

I almost don't know where to begin in describing last night's events in Dallas. The evening was so incredibly moving. So beautifully inspirational. So Team Maddie.

Most amazingly, Team Maddie grew quite a bit larger yesterday. As the evening concluded, the incoming Chairman of the Board – Kevin Cullen – invited the entire roomful of national American Cancer Society volunteers to join Team Maddie. To keep channeling her story as they continue their mission to attack cancer from every angle. As I soaked up the love in the room, I couldn't help but be humbled and overwhelmed by the fact that Maddie continues to inspire. Last night was just a poignant reminder that Maddie's mark on this world is just beginning.

I also want to let you in on a little secret. A secret that I've had to hold tight the last two weeks. But first some context. Last year, at this very same volunteer event, just two months before Maddie was diagnosed with cancer, Grandpa Arnie was introduced as the next Chairman of the Board of the American Cancer Society (yet another coincidence in a long line of coincidences during Maddie's journey). The term for this position was one year. Last night he was therefore scheduled to give his outgoing remarks.

Grandpa's induction speech from last year never quite left me. And as last night's event grew closer, I started writing a new chapter in recognition of the impact Grandpa's speech had on me, and the impact he's had on the Society. Well, upon finishing a draft, my desire to write turned into a vision. A vision of having the opportunity to introduce Grandpa, as well as Maddie, to the American Cancer Society volunteers in Dallas.

With the help of a few special folks within the American Cancer Society leadership, that vision became a reality last night. As I was afforded the privilege of surprising Grandpa Arnie with an introductory speech. My secret? Well, I didn't let Grandpa (or anyone else for that matter) in on the surprise.

After I was seated, Grandpa then followed my introduction with a rousing speech that reminded the entire room what they already knew – that they had a pretty darn special Chairman for the past year.

I won't forget last night for as long as I live. Special thanks to the American Cancer Society for a beautiful evening and for their tireless efforts in the war against cancer. And congratulations again to Grandpa, a true man of action.

Below you can find the full text of my remarks:

One year ago, I was sitting in the audience for this very same event. Only I watched the 2017 Summit not as a volunteer, but as a proud son-in-law with no other connection to cancer, as my father-in-law, Dr. Arnold Baskies (or Grandpa as we call him), was honored as the incoming Chairman of the Board of Directors.

I can still vividly remember two components of Grandpa's epic induction speech. The first, an inspirational call to action where Grandpa challenged us all to be "daring disrupters" to the Society's historic status quo.

I also remember his concluding question to the audience:

"Why volunteer? Why give? Why commit yourself to a 103-year-old, iconic organization?"

As he delivers the answer, he puts a picture on the projection screen. A picture of seven smiling cousins, jumping high into the air above the Long Beach Island sand. On the very left end of this united line of cousinly love, you see a little, adorable, curly-haired girl. Her vertical effort is matched only by her spectacular spirit. Her dancing legs kicked out mid-air, fearlessly ignorant to the painful fall that awaits. That adorable little girl was my two-year-old daughter, Maddie.

With Maddie smiling down on him in the background, Grandpa then provides the answer to his questions. Why volunteer? Why give? Why commit?

Grandpa says, and I quote: "To me, the answer is simple. I would prefer if these folks, our seven grandchildren, will know a world without cancer."

Looking back, the speech almost feels prophetic. Because just two months later, in April 2017, Maddie was diagnosed with a rare cancerous tumor in her spinal cord. Followed by what was supposed to be a year-long chemotherapy regimen.

In lieu of walking you through each chapter of the inspirational eight-and-a-half months that followed, know that this very picture tells the story of her battle. A battle filled with Love. A battle filled with Joy. A family united.

And a little girl high in the air, with her dancing legs kicked out, fearlessly ignorant to the painful fall that awaited.

That fall came on January 4, 2018. The day Maddie's battle with cancer ended all too soon. But as evidenced by my standing at this moment, and by my wife Pammy sitting strong and tall in the audience, Maddie's battle may have ended, but her war – our war – has just begun. And we march forward with Maddie's inspiration, with her fearlessness, and with her spectacular spirit in our hearts.

Today, we come full circle. We return to the annual volunteer meeting. As Grandpa transitions from his impactful term as Chairman. Reflecting on Grandpa's leadership role in the fight against cancer, I offer three simple words:

Man. Of. Action.

What is a Man of Action, you ask? If you see Grandpa smiling, it's because we used this term frequently in the final two weeks of Maddie's own battle. The final weeks carried us through a litany of medical professionals from administrators to nurses to doctors. To pass the time (and frankly, just to think about something else), Grandpa and I would categorize these individuals into one of two pods: those who were men and women of action, and those who were not. Those who preferred to pontificate and passively ponder on the problem at hand. And the people of action. The people on the ground. The human propellers. The do-ers. The daring disrupters.

The war against cancer needs more men and women of action. They need more of you. And tonight I have the privilege of standing here in honor of our family's boldest representation of this movement. As he passes the

Chairman baton to the trusted, active hands of Kevin Cullen.

Congratulations, Grandpa, on a daringly disruptive year of service. The Society is blessed for your involvement. We are blessed to call you our own. And I just know that adorable little girl is still smiling down on you in the background.

The Role of Inspirer (2/8/18)

Prior to the American Cancer Society's main event, we decided to pick one tourist destination in Dallas to experience during the day. After a little research, we went with the Sixth Floor Museum at Dealey Plaza. The museum dedicated to presenting the life, death, and legacy of President John F. Kennedy.

The museum experience was deeply moving. And certain aspects hit home particularly hard. As we entered the museum, one of the first exhibits explained how Jackie O's fateful visit to Dallas in November 1963 represented her very first public appearance since the death of her newborn child.

Fifty-five years later, there we stood. In Dallas. In this museum. As a precursor to our first (and only) public presentation about Maddie just one month after her passing.

Amidst the political backdrop and the conspiracies, I was simply taken aback by the pure inspiration of President Kennedy's words. Various examples of live video and audio footage graced the museum speakers. And I realized just how woefully short the world seems to be on inspirational voices in this day and age. Without comment on either political party, politics has become less about the politics of inspiration and more about the politics of consternation and aggravation. And so as I walked through the museum, filled with the inspiration of President Kennedy's wise and strengthening words, Pammy pointed out the following quote on the wall by Historian Daniel Boorstin:

> "To those who have the misfortune to die young, history assigns the role of inspirer."

Although Mr. Boorstin wasn't talking about Maddie, I couldn't help but make my way down the sixth floor stairwell with Maddie's inspiration on my mind. In her three and a half years on this Earth, Maddie has already inspired more people than most of us will in a lifetime. Because that is who she was. That is who she is. The girl who was dancing while cancering. The incomparable inspirer.

Only here is what I also know. History does not write itself. And so I consider it my duty to carry Maddie's torch. To continue to be the voice for her inspirational message. To continue to give life to the girl who – despite no longer walking this physical Earth – appears to breathe life into others effortlessly. To continue to rally and grow Team Maddie.

In many ways, this next phase of our journey is just an adaptation of my parental duties. As Lily's parents, Pammy and I owe Lily an obligation to keep her loved. To keep her safe. To keep her enriched. To keep her happy. As Maddie's parents, our job did not end just because January 4th came and went. Instead, we still have a job to do for Maddie. To keep her in our memories. To keep her in our hearts. To keep telling her story. To inspire others. To save others. To teach others. To keep Maddie as Maddie, at least in our hearts and minds. To ensure her assignment to the role of inspirer. History aside, Maddie deserves nothing less.

Miracle Update (2/9/18)

No sooner did Pammy and I return from Dallas than did we learn that we have been invited to speak at the American Cancer Society's premier fundraising event in Chicago. The event – called "Discovery Ball" – is one of the largest nonprofit events in the city. The theme for the Society's annual campaign this year is "attacking cancer from every angle." We have been designated as the keynote speaker to represent the angle of a caregiver.

The coincidences and meaning associated with the event are too hard to ignore. For one, my thirty-two-year-old sister, Amy, is the Society employee responsible for organizing this event. Even before Grandpa Arnie was the Chairman of the Board for the Society, Amy began her impactful career for the American Cancer Society over five years ago. She worked her way up from planning Relays for Life to organizing a young professionals annual event to now leading the charge on Discovery Ball.

And this year, of all years, Amy is creating the event taking place on, of all days, April 21st. The day when B.C. became A.C. The day of Maddie's six-hour surgery. And now one year later – to the day – Pammy and I will have the opportunity to share the privilege of being Maddie's caregiver, and hopefully continue to shine her inspirational light, at an event led by Maddie's aunt and my sister.

Needless to say, the opportunity is a true honor in the highest of regards. I just hope to do my sister proud. To do Maddie proud. And to play my part to help attack cancer from every angle. I'm certainly on my way. Immediately after Amy asked Pammy and me to speak, I took to my keyboard. Without anything but the theme of the Society's annual campaign in my head, and Maddie in my heart, the words flowed from my fingertips faster than anything I've written before. The speech (which I'll wait to reveal until April 21st) is a beautiful tribute to Maddie and an inspirational call to action for the Society volunteers. But perhaps most appropriately, it's written as a duet. An inspirational dance of sorts. For both me and Pammy to share in together. Indeed, April 21st is a long way away. But then again, both now and for the rest of our lives, April 21st of any year will always be close by. Reminding us that our job on this Earth is not yet over.

Miracle Update (2/15/18)

The process for legally forming our charitable entity is under way. With the advice of trusted counsel, we are going to begin the organization in the form of a charitable trust. In doing so, the drafting process requires us to confirm two aspects of the project: 1) the full legal name; and 2) the charitable purpose.

With respect to the name, we learned that we are encouraged to send a signal to future participants that the organization is a charitable one. As a result, adding the word "foundation" to the name is most common. We toyed with "The Dancing While Cancering Foundation," but the formality watered down the concept too much for us. That said, we could appreciate how "Dancing While Cancering" alone – without any further markers – doesn't necessarily signal the charitable nature of our cause.

Something else was missing too. As we proceed with plans to build this beautiful charitable mission, we do not want to lose sight of its spiritual inspirer. The true toddler foundation of the Foundation. And with that thought, our full name was born:

Dancing While Cancering
The Maddie Kramer Foundation

I smile just retyping those words. The words need no interpretation. They say it all. From there, deriving our charitable purpose was equally natural. The mission?

Bringing joy to the inpatient hospital experience for children with cancer.

Concise. Impactful. Unique. And vintage Maddie. Who better to help bring joy to the inpatient cancer experience than the girl who spent her entire battle dancing while cancering? Our task will be to take that mission and transform it into real life impact. Once the foundation is up and running, we currently envision two main ways to bring joy to this inspiring world:

First, through welcome packages for new pediatric oncology patients filled with items to promote joy during the inpatient hospital experience: items such as a wireless speaker, decorations, window decals, and musical instruments.

Second, through projects to improve recreational spaces and opportunities on the pediatric oncology hospital floors.

Make no mistake, these initial ideas are just scratching the surface. If there were any doubt before, I am now only further convinced that Maddie's story, and Maddie's impact on this world, is just beginning. The beautiful dance of her life will be endless. And it is an honor, and a privilege, to help keep that dance going. We love you, sweet girl.

Lily's Morning Message (2/21/18)

Every morning, I experience the blessing of being able to open Lily's door. And to see her smiling face as my first human contact before starting each day. What a gift. Maddie's good morning alarm was soft and soul warming: "Daaaaaadddddyyyyy, cooooooome geeeeeet meeeee." Lily hits me in a different, but no less meaningful, way. She greets my entrance with a full-fledged, vintage Lily convulsive clap and smile session. It doesn't get much better than that to start a day.

And the Lily Show doesn't stop there either. After I lift her from the crib, Lily immediately turns to her purple wall. First, she waves feverishly at her colorful butterfly decals. Then she turns and waves to her penguin painting. Then to her bubblegum clock. Then to her blinds. Then to a picture sitting on her shelf. A picture of a laughing Lily with a miraculous Maddie.

Lily rises. She claps. And she welcomes the world around her with a wave and a smile.

Rise. Clap. Welcome the world with a wave and a smile.

Per usual, Lily is onto something. As you can imagine, my morning mind is not always silent these days. While we were blessed to move through the trauma phase of Maddie's passing on the strength of our family, friends, and community, that doesn't mean our thoughts are always pain-free. But then Lily reminds me of the path forward. She reminds me of the lens through which to view the world. Through her little eyes, I see our new morning narrative. Rise. Clap. Welcome the world with a wave and a smile. This daily dance with Lily keeps me upright each morning. Keeps me choosing life. Keeps me moving forward.

And so goes each morning. I refuse to give into the darkness. The same mental abyss that floated around us during Maddie's cancer treatment remains today albeit in a different form. How do you put one foot in front of the other in a world filled with tragedy? Well, the walk through each day might be long, but I am at least confident how to start each morning.

Rise. Clap. Welcome the world with a wave and a smile.

Miracle Update (3/9/18)

D ancing While Cancering is continuing to take form. This past week, Pammy and I met with three different graphic design companies. Companies that could help take our concept and derive a beautiful logo that encapsulates our Maddie-driven purpose and to deliver a website that provides a vehicle to view our desired impact on the world. From soup to nuts, the creation process will take somewhere between three to four months. In the meantime, Pammy and I just want to be sure that we select a true dance partner in this mission. Someone who feels the meaning behind Dancing While Cancering. Someone who hears Maddie's story and finds beauty in the dance steps she left behind. Fortunately, I think that we're on our way. As all three professionals not only appeared technologically inclined but emotionally equipped. We'll take a few weeks to make a decision, but for now, our dance continues.

The only not-so-minor Foundation detail hanging out there? We still need to make sure that we have a "dance party" venue for our Foundation endeavors. A place to bring our Maddie-inspired mission. A place to spread her joy. Without question, we hope that our first waltz will be at Lurie's Place. We're hoping to set up time to chat with the powers that be in the next couple of weeks. Hopefully more good news awaits.

Spring Forward (3/10/18)

S pring Forward. A little more sunshine in each day. I like the sound of that. Fortunately, springing forward and holding on to more and more sunshine each day is exactly what Pammy and I have been doing these past few months. While there is a long list of contributing power sources for this positive propulsion, there is no doubt as to the two biggest drivers: Maddie and Lily. Our two Miracles and Lights still keeping us going.

Lily grows more smiley by the day. And when those two lonely front-bottom teeth peek out surrounded by a pair of pudge-packed cheeks, all is right in the world. As Lily's eyes get bluer and her hair gets blonder with each passing day, only her stork's address remains in question. Because her love, her hope, and her light are absolutely unambiguous.

Meanwhile, Maddie remains a force of positivity. It seems that wherever we go these days, someone is relaying the inspirational impact that Maddie has had on their life. Nearly every ounce of our post-January pain is pried away by the countervailing privilege of being Maddie's parents. Besides the indelible personal mark Maddie has left on the people around her, she has Pammy and me springing forward into sunnier days.

Most recently, we learned that Lurie's Place has officially approved the initial idea that Pammy and I have been planning to shine Maddie's light. The concept? Creating "Maddie's Character Closet" in the 17th Floor Playroom. Soon enough, the other tiny heroes toddling around the 17th Floor will be supported by the same animated pals that joined Maddie on her journey. On April 19th (nearly one year from the day I first placed a curly-haired, previously healthy Maddie on the Lurie's Place scale in triage), with Maddie in our hearts, Pammy and I will be stocking the Lurie's Place playroom closet shelves with fourteen figurine "families," each housed in individual containers just how Maddie would've liked it. After all, what's Lurie's Place without Daniel, Peppa, Doc, and the rest of the imaginative gang?

Equally exciting, this cancer-resistant character clan wouldn't have been possible without Team Maddie. On June 26, 2018 – Maddie's birthday – Lurie's Place will be honoring Maddie with a plaque that formally designates the closet space publicly as "Maddie's Character Closet." The dedication will take place in the small, intimate walls of the 17th Floor Playroom with our immediate family as well as the doctors and nurses who helped make the joy Maddie brought us all this past year possible. It's particularly special to know that if we're ever looking to find Maddie in Lurie's Place, she will be in the 17th Floor Playroom. Commemorating her characters. Combatting cancer and chemo with creativity.

Where does Team Maddie come into play? The minimum donation to memorialize this hospital space with a plaque is $25,000. In lieu of requiring a one-time donation in the amount of $25,000, however, the generous folks at Lurie's Place offered to count every single dollar raised by Team Maddie since her birthday last June toward that threshold. As of a few days ago, wouldn't you know what the exact dollar amount that our amazing team generated? $24,999.

Thanks to you, as we spring forward toward sunnier days, Maddie will still be bringing her sunshine to the 17th Floor. Still bringing smiles. Still bringing joy. Still bringing imagination. Still bringing love.

As I told many of you in January, Maddie's story is only just beginning. And we just know there is more sunshine to come. With Maddie and Lily continuing to spring us forward.

<u>Go Go Go (3/18/18)</u>

A few weeks after her first birthday, Lily is still a little girl of few words. But the meaning packed in those words never ceases to amaze me. Beyond the expected, typical baby babbles of "Mama" and "Dada," Lily consistently turns to this mantra of mobility every time we make our way toward the front door:

Go Go Go!

I have to admit, the chugging-like sound that gurgles out of her little mouth alone is worth the price of emission. But I also find that Lily's not-so-little exit song is like our own little engine that could.

Go Go Go!

Those three words tell the tale of our Lily-led treatment. Cancer did everything it could to slow us down. Yet we will not, and we cannot, stop going. *Go Go Go* is our cure. *Go Go Go* is our goal. *Go Go Go* is our answer. We go to preschool with Lily. We go to synagogue. We go to Lurie's Place to give back. We go consult with intellectual property attorneys. We go visit with charitable advisors. We go to work. We go to the grocery store. We go for coffee. We go for doughnuts. We go out to dinner. We go to the park. We go spend time with friends. We go spend time with family.

We go.

Or in the words of Lily, we *Go Go Go!*

I can imagine immobility and inertia being two major forces after an unimaginable loss like we experienced. But just as Maddie never stopped going, neither shall we. That doesn't mean we are necessarily moving in the same way or without challenge. Change is to be expected. Difficulty is to be expected. At least for me and Pammy, however, just the act of go go going is proving curative. There is purpose in movement. There is life in movement. There is no quit in movement. And we are not stopping any time soon. The tapping of my fingers along this very same keyboard that held my hands through life A.C. tells the story. The same story as Lily's enlivening lullaby.

Go Go Go.

Miracle Update (3/22/18)

Go Go Go is right, Lil! It's been quite a stretch of Go Go Go for all things *Maddie's Miracles* and Dancing While Cancering. In the past week, we've identified a book cover creator for *Maddie's Miracles*, finalized a critical round of revisions to the manuscript, selected a website and logo designer for the Foundation, prepared a first draft of the Foundation's governing documents, reached out to prospective nonprofit accounting firms, and perhaps most importantly, we received confirmation from some of our favorite people at Lurie's Place that they officially have given us a green light on the Foundation's mission and look forward to partnering with us on all things joy-creation within the hospital walls. And yes, we're still trying to raise a now 13-month-old child and hold down our day jobs.

[Exhale].

I'm writing this entry somewhere around 3:30 a.m. on a Thursday morning. I haven't felt the urge to write at this time of day, let alone been awake to write at this time of day, since my sleepovers at Lurie's Place. But my mind is motivated by moving ahead on Maddie's eternal miracles.

With every passing day, and with every passing task, I only grow more confident that these ventures will be impactful. That Maddie will continue to make her mark. And that she will continue to live on as an inspiration.

Go Go Go!

Reframing the Question (4/2/18)

This past weekend was the Passover holiday. Which is highlighted by a festive family meal that is a combination of a celebratory gathering and a somber reminder of the Jewish people's B.C. (yes, the literal B.C.) freedom from slavery in Egypt. I'll spare you any in-depth biblical interpretations. But one of the cornerstones of the Passover holiday is the asking of the "Four Questions." The cornerstone question of these cornerstone questions is this:

Why is this night different from all other nights?

As Jewish families across the country gather with their families around a dining room table chock-full of food, they are all asking this annual question. Unfortunately, any spiritual or religious purpose behind the question was lost on me this year. Nearly three months since Maddie left our physical world, the flood of differences on this Passover night drowned my mind. Looking across our long and otherwise full table, the difference was stark. Loving family member after loving family member. But nowhere to be found was that unforgettable smile. Nowhere to be heard was that sweet, sing-songy voice. Nowhere to be seen were those dancing legs. In a holiday dedicated to celebrating the freedom from affliction, I couldn't have felt the pain of missing Maddie more.

In these somber moments post-January, I occasionally get stuck in the rut of asking my least favorite question. A question that is not supposed to be posed over our Passover plates.

Why Maddie?

It's the most painful question of the A.C. questions. I remember this question dominating my mind in the initial stages after April 21, 2017. But with Maddie's miraculous recovery, she pulled us all out of the mental persecution of this problematic question. We didn't have to consume ourselves with the hurt of *Why Maddie?*, as we were instead consumed with the amazement of Maddie's progress. *Why Maddie?* quickly became *Why, Maddie!* As the first quarter of 2018 ticks by, however, my mind is now turning back the clock. My brain rewinds to that April 21st question of persecution. The ticking clock of this perse-question clicks, clacks, ticks, and tocks again in my thoughts.

Why Maddie?
Why Maddie?
Why Maddie?

I have no doubt that my psychological freedom does not lie in continued questioning. Nor can I find freedom in attempting to answer. After all, what answer could possibly be satisfying? Perhaps the pre-determinists of us are tempted to say, "This was Maddie's purpose. She had a greater good to achieve on this Earth." True or not, I could never bring myself to swallow the bitter pill that Maddie's existence, and most especially her suffering – and our suffering — were somehow a necessary remedy for any alleged societal shortcomings. Her story could have carried a different ending — one that also included her carrying her incredible spirit into a meaningful adulthood — and still yielded the same, if not greater, result. Maddie represented everything beautiful about this world. She was exuberance personified. And the intense void she has left in this world — irrespective of theoretical purposes — only causes me to further wallow in *Why Maddie?*

So on this Passover holiday, on an occasion filled with the Four Questions, I am not turning to questions. Nor am I turning to answers. I'm instead turning to statements. To facts. To indisputable reality. When *Why Maddie?* starts to batter my brain, I am going to boast beauty. And allow *Why Maddie?* to become *Maddie is why.* Because while I will never satisfactorily answer *Why Maddie?*, I am filled with the fantastic fuel that finishes off the statement *Maddie is why.*

Maddie is why I get up in the morning thinking of how I can make the world around me a better place.

Maddie is why Pammy and I have committed ourselves to creating a charitable organization dedicated to spreading joy where many see hardship.

Maddie is why we hope to share a story of light and a story of love in a way that makes a difference in someone else's life in need of sunshine.

Maddie is why a hospital became a place to play, to dance, and to imagine.

Maddie is why a community became a family.

Maddie is why a family became a team.

Maddie is why I am who I am today. And why I continue to strive to be better.

Maddie is why yet again we are flipping the narrative. And instead of posing a question…instead of electing to wallow in sorrow…we are moving forward with fire. The fire of the most inspirational human being I've ever met. The fire of freedom from questions. The fire of focusing on moving forward. With Maddie as my answer and not my question.

From Hope to Action (4/6/18)

In Hebrew, the word "Yizkor" means "Remember." And four times per year, synagogues across the world hold special Yizkor services as an opportunity for mourners to remember their loved ones. One of those four services takes place every year on the last day of Passover. Today was that day. A day of Yizkor. A day to remember.

Pammy and I walked into the Temple Sholom Yizkor service around 10:30 a.m. We were the youngest mourners in the room probably by 30 years. Just another stark reminder of the harsh reality of Maddie's passing. Fortunately, as with all things Maddie, that harsh reality quickly gave way to prayers of light and hope. Mind you, very few people in this room knew Maddie. Very few people in this room knew me and Pammy. And certainly the clergy speaking had no idea we would be in attendance, as there was no formal or informal RSVP.

Yet after hearing even just five minutes of the Rabbi's thoughtful words, you would have thought his analysis was pre-scripted to illustrate where Pammy and I were in the grieving process. That someone was wire-tapping my ongoing internal writings. The similarities in messaging were astounding.

The Rabbi first spoke of the concept of slavery. The idea of bondage. Not just literal enslavement embodied in the Passover holiday. But the chains that we all carry. Whether psychological chains, emotional burdens, or just mental musings, many of us are pulled down by some form of mind-driven weight. And that just as the Passover holiday generally celebrates the end of the Jewish people's literal slavery in Egypt, the last day of Passover – this Yizkor – invites us to also put down our psychological chains. The weights that have been burdening us over the course of the year.

For the mourners in the room, the Rabbi focused on the most critical transition we can make as Passover concludes. The healthiest way to remember. The most constructive way to deconstruct the chains. He said the following:

Now is the time to go from Hope to Action.

I was floored. Hope to Action as a key to freedom? Is this Rabbi consulting Lily? Transforming her *Go Go Go* sermon into more formal spiritual guidance? Yet again, as with all things Maddie and Lily, I can't explain the coincidence, but I will draw every drop of meaning. To be sure, Pammy and I have been running with this key to freedom for weeks now. Ready to open the next hope-inspired door. At this very moment, on this very Yizkor, we are standing at the front gates of our very transition from Hope to Action. Because starting on April 19th, our dreams of making a difference start to become a reality. As we remember Maddie, we'll be taking all of her light, all of her joy, and all of her hope, and transforming them all to action.

As we walk through that Hope to Action gate, the first door we open will be the door to a character closet. Maddie's Character Closet. A literal and symbolic home of hope that we are creating within the Lurie's Place walls. One day later, we'll continue our walk into the "Hall of Hope," one of the main attractions at the American Cancer Society's Discovery Ball event. With hope in our hearts, Pammy and I will be leading a call to action. A call to raise money to continue the Society's ongoing war in the battle against cancer. A war that will then continue not with weapons. But with the awareness bursting from the soon-to-be-published pages of *Maddie's Miracles*, and the joy that Dancing While Cancering will bring to the pediatric cancer world.

As the Rabbi calls us to move forward, Pammy and I are literally standing on the precipice of Hope to Action. Gripping tightly our keys to freedom. In our hope-filled hands. With Maddie in our hearts. On this Yizkor, we remember Maddie. She continues to inspire. But just as important, she continues to call us to action.

Ode to an Artist (4/12/18)

Today, the artist we commissioned to create the cover for *Maddie's Miracles* sent us his final product. Upon hiring, he asked me and Pammy to pass along our thoughts and ideas, so that he could take them into account while he tackled the project. As you can imagine, I drafted a lengthy description regarding the themes of the book, the emotions we hoped to evoke, and the ideal imagery for any cover page. The instructions that only an OCD attorney could craft. Sparing you my treatise-like guidance, suffice it to say that Peter – our trusted cover creator who had never met us before, had never known Maddie, and was doing this on a contract basis – did what any good customer service-oriented artist awaiting his contingency fee would do…

He ignored me completely!

Leave it to a true artist to paint outside the lines. And better yet, the result was just awe-inspiring. Although there's no substitute for seeing the actual image of the cover firsthand, its warming presence is palpable. The gentle, soft colors are as calming as a bedside evening waltz with Maddie snuggled into my shoulder. For someone who had not read the story, or followed Maddie's journey, the imagery and symbolism was coincidentally striking. A quiet, beautiful view of the Moana-like horizon line where the sky meets the sea. The thin black line hovering above the water reminds us that it's always darkest before the dawn. That while the thin black line of cancer was always hovering above our lives, the black line was never our focal point. Never a dominant player in our game of life.

Instead, the awe-inspiring natural beauty of the surrounding sweet sea and sunshine take the main stage on this cover page (just as Maddie's sweetness and light navigated us through our narrative). With the purity and light that was Maddie dominating this otherwise still, seaside setting, you'll also find a few, select images in motion. Images rising above the thin black line. Moving forward with the beauty of the light gracing their journey.

Those few images? None other than *three little birds*.

For those of you who don't necessarily have *Maddie's Miracles* at the tip of your memory banks, one of Maddie's main theme songs in the early days of her diagnosis was Bob Marley's *Three Little Birds*. So as me, Pammy, and Lily attempt to soar onward and upward – telling one another that "every little thing is gonna be alright" – we do so with Maddie's beautiful light warming our souls. And with Lily leading our flock of three away from the darkness.

Thank you, Peter, for capturing the beauty of Maddie's story all on one page. And for warmly inviting our readers into the gift that is her life.

Lokai Days (4/14/18)

S oon after Maddie's diagnosis, Uncle Mikey Boy and Aunt Risa sent me and Pammy a set of "Lokai" bracelets. The bracelets are made up of rubber beads. The bracelets come in all different colors for all different charitable causes. But no matter which bracelet you have, two of the beads are always specifically colored – one black and one white.

The white bead is filled with water from Mt. Everest, the highest point on earth. The black bead is filled with mud from the Dead Sea, the lowest point on Earth. The Lokai packaging reminds you of its mindful message of balance: when you're on top of the world, remember to stay humble. To stay grateful. When you're on the bottom, stay hopeful. Keep going. Our ups and downs are transient. Forever cyclical. This little circular bracelet lets us in on the secret lore of searching for balance in an inevitably imbalanced life.

With Maddie on my mind, and a bright yellow Lokai on my wrist, Pammy and I are entering our "Lokai Days." This next weekend represents the one-year anniversary of one of the lowest of our lows. On April 20, 2017, one year ago from this upcoming Friday, Maddie and I walked into the Lurie Children's Hospital Emergency Room thinking that she had virus. The 48 hours that followed sucked us into the depths of darkness that no Dead Sea mud could match. Without question, the emotionality of the upcoming week has been sitting in my stomach. Glued to my gut. Bonded to my breath. Tied to my tears. Laying on my Lokai'd left wrist.

But just as in April 2017, Pammy and I will not wallow in sorrow for April 2018. We're turning the black bead of our bracelet downward in favor of the pure white bead of hope. We're spending these Lokai Days drinking from the cup of inspiration. And there will be multiple gulps of gratitude. The week of memorializing the miracle that is Maddie begins on Wednesday, April 18th. Just a few days ago, one of the employees of the Lurie's Place fundraising arm notified me and Pammy that the parental speaker at one of their upcoming events had canceled. In need of some parental positivity, they turned to me and Pammy to gauge our interest. Without batting an eye, we said yes. What better way to kick off our Lokai Days than to let this group of Lurie supporters in on the legend and love of Maddie.

Our efforts to climb our emotional Mt. Everest continue on Thursday, April 19th. When Pammy and I will return to the 17th Floor Playroom with about fourteen figurine families by our side. Figurine families who figure to bring joy to, and befriend, a bevy of battling heroes. This memorial and impactful respite will be our longest stay at Lurie's Place since the lowest of our lows just a few months ago. Cleansing the memories of those muddier challenges with the Everest-worthy waters of hope.

That hope then reaches its peak on Saturday, April 21st. One year – to the day – from Maddie's MRI results. When a black and white image charred our previously pure perspectives. On Saturday, we aim to make Maddie's forward-looking purpose in this world equally black and white. As Pammy and I take the stage to share Maddie's spirit with hundreds of American Cancer Society supporters at one of the city's largest nonprofit fundraisers.

Ever since April 2017, Maddie showed us the way out of the darkness. She miraculously washed away all of our Dead Sea mud with her months and months of hope, love, and inspiration. With my bright yellow Lokai on my wrist, and Maddie in our hearts, we will tackle these Lokai Days with the same beautiful formula.

Sharing the Cup of Inspiration (4/18/18)

Our beginning efforts to tackle these Lokai Days got off to a special and meaningful start. The event this evening was attended by a group of young professionals who call themselves "The Lurie Children's Innovators." These dedicated, aspiring philanthropists each committed – as part of joining this group – $5,000 per member to a specific project within the hospital. After raising a collective $150,000, their first meeting took place in January, at which point they voted on the project to receive their donations. They agreed to invest in "Precision Medicine for Cancer Care," which – in essence – is a more tailored and less toxic method of treating certain childhood cancers.

Tonight was their first meeting since making their project selection. And the speakers included parents (me and Pammy), an oncologist (Dr. Stewart Goldman at Lurie Children's), and one of the leading Precision Medicine researchers at the hospital (Dr. Amy Walz). The goal was to give the Innovators a sense of the reach of their impact. And to see the faces behind their good deeds.

In order to kick off the night, the emcee – Grant Stirling – tried to rally this group of young, motivated peers. Without any background on our prepared remarks, he explained how the night promised to be filled with a cool venue, cool people, and a cool project. It was a fun kickoff for a millennial-filled crowd. With that backdrop, Pammy and I took to the microphone. I'm not sure if we fulfilled the coolness of the mission, but we certainly did a memorable job of shining Maddie's light. It was a special, beautiful evening, and we met some wonderful and supportive people in the process. Maddie's presence was everywhere and inspiring to all of those in the room.

Below are our remarks (some prepared and some not so prepared):

Good evening, everyone. Grant promised you all a night filled with cool people. Well, what Grant didn't tell you is that I am the *Understudy of Cool*. The original parent speaker for tonight had to cancel last Thursday. And so Pammy and I received the invitation just a few days ago. Rumor has it the originally scheduled speaker was tall, handsome, strong, inspirational, and witty.

Well, you got me instead, so…

I hope you enjoy your food!

On a serious note, thank you – the Lurie Children's Innovators – for the incredible commitment you've made to a place that's very near and dear to our hearts. While you might have some sense of the impact you're having on the patients, what you don't know is the impact that you're having on me and Pammy tonight. And what an especially meaningful time it is for us to spend an evening with you.

Pammy and I are about to begin what we're calling our "Lokai Days." How many of you have heard of the company "Lokai"?

[No one raises their hand].

This is not a plug. We don't work for the company. Lokai makes customized beaded bracelets. The bracelets come in a variety of colors in honor of various charitable causes. But regardless of bracelet color, there is one constant in each bracelet. Each bracelet has one white bead that contains water from Mt. Everest, the highest point on earth. And one black bead that contains mud from the Dead Sea, the lowest point on earth.

The message behind these bracelets is to encourage us to always maintain balance in our lives. Whenever we're looking out from those Mt. Everest moments, when it seems like work couldn't be more prosperous, when life couldn't be more amazing, remember to stay humble. To stay grateful. Remember the dark days that preceded those light moments. Remember those who are not blessed with such a beautiful view and are instead on their own Dead Sea swim. And on the flip side, when you're in those Dead Sea moments, remember to keep going. To keep swimming. Because you never know when that moment of hope might come. When you might be able to swim toward the top of the water again.

I've been wearing a Lokai bracelet since April 2017. My bracelet is yellow. In honor of childhood cancer awareness. And in memory of our late three-year-old daughter, Maddie.

Pammy and I refer to these upcoming days as our Lokai Days because they're the essence of our strive for balance. Days where we are reminded of our lowest of the lows, but where we try to lift ourselves up by drinking from the cup of inspiration (and maybe from a glass of wine or two). To engage in charitable activities. To surround ourselves with inspirational people. And so when the hospital reached out to us last week to join you tonight, despite the short notice, we didn't hesitate to say yes.

Because in two days, we're forced to remember the first anniversary of one of the two lowest of our Lokai Days. The day I walked into the Lurie Children's Hospital Emergency Room with Maddie thinking that she just had a cold. That swollen lymph nodes were causing pain in her neck and difficulty moving. We were otherwise in one of those Mt. Everest moments of our lives. Maddie was everything you could ever ask for in a daughter. She was sweet, she was funny, she was smart, she loved playing, singing, dancing…and you couldn't help but just smile in her presence. And so when we walked into the emergency room, it started off like any other fun night. Maddie had a juice box in one hand and a bag of animal crackers in the other. We watched *Lion Guard* on the waiting room television.

When they called Maddie into triage, I put her on the scale. Her legs buckled under her. In a matter of hours, pain and paralysis took over. Sometime around midnight on April 21st – one year ago from Saturday – we learned the reason why. That a rare, cancerous tumor was filling four levels of Maddie's little spinal cord. A tumor that affects 30-50 new patients per year. Only 2% of which first appear in the spinal cord only. 2% of 30-50 children. That's less than one child per year. In 2017, that child was our daughter, Maddie. You can't even imagine the depths of our dive into the Dead Sea mud that accompanied coming to grips with that reality.

But, because of the folks at this amazing institution, we didn't have to stay there for very long. We were able to keep swimming.

Thanks to Dr. Alden, a neurosurgeon at Lurie Children's, Maddie's tumor – despite being located in one of the most delicate parts of the body – was removed with the precision of an artist. And in a matter of weeks, Maddie went from a complete inability to walk to going back to dancing, smiling, singing, laughing, running, and jumping like we would never have imagined.

Thanks to Dr. Stew's Brain Tumor Team, and led by our incredible oncologist, Dr. Fangusaro, despite a disease that most hospitals across the country have never seen before – let alone have the capability to diagnose and treat – Maddie was able to undergo a formal treatment protocol. We were able to keep swimming. She was able to keep battling.

Thanks to the child life specialists, Maddie's battle continued, but not with your typical weapons of war. Maddie was able to fight her battle with toys, games, music, dancing, princesses, the incredible 17th Floor Playroom, iPads, Frozen castles, and smiles.

Thanks to Lurie Children's, we spent eight-and-a-half beautiful months overlooking a glorious Mt. Everest-like view unlike anything we'll ever see in our life. Even though the mud from the Dead Sea was still all around us.

Unfortunately, the second of our Lokai Days came earlier this year. On January 4, 2018. When Maddie's battle with cancer ended all too soon. But Pammy and I made a commitment to ourselves that day. A commitment that Maddie's life would be remembered not as a tragedy but as an inspiration. A commitment that Maddie would live on through our actions. Through every donation. Through every hopeful conversation. Through every act of inspiration.

So please know that simply by being here tonight you are already playing your part in keeping one little girl and her beautiful memory alive. And with the commitment you've made to Lurie Children's, you're making strides to save lives. To eliminating these Lokai Days from future parents' calendars. And to improving the care for this devastating disease.

Wherever your life takes you, do not lose the spirit of philanthropy that brings you all together this evening. From my view, that philanthropic spirit is the essence of the balance embodied in my bracelet. Whether you are in a Mt. Everest point of life, or a Dead Sea period, philanthropy reminds you of the others who are struggling on their swim for life. And you are choosing to shine the lights of hope, inspiration, and charity on their darkness.

Keep up the incredible work. Thank you for your commitment. And thank you for allowing us to share this special evening with you.

Pure Imagination (4/19/18)

Two days ago, Pammy and I sat down with our logo and website designer, Mark. The purpose of the meeting was to start to fuel him with the feelings behind the foundation. To help fill him with the spirit of Maddie in a way that would spur ideas for logo and web design. Foundation matters aside, the meeting itself was so very special. Just having the opportunity to talk about Maddie. About everything she meant to us. About everything she left with us. About what we hope to share with others in her memory. The conversation alone made for a meaningful day.

Being just as much a web artist as a web designer, Mark also asked some thought-provoking questions. The one that stuck with me the most? "Which famous person (real or fiction) best represents Maddie?" Pammy and I threw around variety of names. But one of them really hit me:

Willy Wonka.

No sooner did we say the name than did I hear the sound of *Pure Imagination*. The soothing lyrics gently flowing from ear to ear:

There is no life I know
To compare with pure imagination
Living there, you'll be free, if you truly wish to be

If that doesn't represent Maddie, and the beauty of life with her A.C., I don't know what does. Of all of Maddie's incredible characteristics (of which there were many), none were more critical to our collective course through cancer than her creative mind. Almost every feel good Maddie morning started off the same way. With her coming downstairs and picking out the two most crucial parts to the day: which house and which character family...

"Daddy, I'll have the purple house and the Daniel characters."

"Grandma, I want the Peppa house and the Peppa characters."

"Mommy, let's play with Anna and Elsa and the Frozen castle."

Without question, there was no life we knew that would compare with Maddie's pure imagination. Living there, watching her dive headfirst into her character world, we were all free. Free from fear. Free from sadness. Free from the what-ifs. Free from the what could be. In Maddie's world of her creation, there was no cancer. Just Daniel. And Peppa. And Doc. And Dory. And the hundreds of other characters neatly organized into the piles of Ziploc bags lining our playroom closet.

Maddie's imaginative world was at its ultimate peak during our final couple of weeks at Lurie's Place. I'll never forget our explorative journeys around the holidays. During our sleepovers, we would go on scavenger hunts across the floor. Looking out for scary animals along the way. Pointing out hidden treasures on the walls. And at some point on our journey, Maddie decided that we had a destination. The name?

Shani Bakani.

It has a magical ring to it, no? *Shani Bakani.* If you've never heard of the *Shani Bakani* it's because it doesn't exist. Maddie made it up. Her three-year-old imaginative mind just wanted to give us a new destination to seek out during our 17th Floor explorations. Despite discovering every nook and cranny of the 17th Floor, however, Maddie never let me find the *Shani Bakani.* But like all things Maddie, it's never really been about the destination. It has only been about the walk. The walk side by side with the most beautifully imaginative little girl I've ever met.

That walk continues today.

With Maddie by our spiritual side, we re-entered the 17th Floor Playroom with the gift she shared with all of us: her imaginative play. Welcomed by a group of Maddie's favorite nurses, we collectively compiled fourteen individual containers of character clans. Each with its own customized, colorful label courtesy of our cousin and newfound C.O.O. of Maddie's Character Closet, Ali Fishman. As we filled up each imaginative container, our hearts simultaneously filled with memories and love of Maddie. And a playroom that was so influential in her ability to turn the Ann & Robert H. Lurie Children's Hospital of Chicago into Lurie's Place.

A couple of hours, a few tears, and lots of smiles later, Pammy and I were able to stand before a soon-to-be-dedicated "Maddie's Character Closet" in complete awe. We both couldn't help but wonder how Maddie would've reacted to this slice of character heaven. But we could certainly smile at the possibilities. What an incredible legacy for Maddie to leave in her favorite playroom. We have no doubt that her light will be shining brightly in those colorful, character-filled containers. Fueling the imagination of our future heroes for years to come.

Hall of Hope (4/22/18)

Last night was the 2018 American Cancer Society Discovery Ball. The final lap of our Lokai Days marathon on the anniversary of perhaps the darkest of our 2017 memories: April 21st. But this year, we were not pacing around an operating room hallway. Instead, we were greeted with "The Hall of Hope." Upon entering the gala, you're welcomed by this inspirational "hallway" that is comprised of several personalized floor-to-ceiling banners that line the room and portray photos and details of the various "Impact Makers" who would be sharing their stories for the evening. Researchers. Survivors. Doctors. Caregivers. And our family. Led by Maddie, the most inspirational of Impact Makers that I'll ever lay eyes on.

As we proceeded from the Hall of Hope into the main event, the ballroom was just stunning. Not surprisingly, my sister – Amy – exceeded all expectations for the level of breathtaking beauty backdropping an inspirational evening. When it was all said and done, the Discovery Ball raised over $3,000,000 to help continue the fight against cancer. $3,000,000. Quite a number. And quite an event. Congratulations, Amy, and thank you for making us a part of such a special night.

As for our words, Pammy and I did our best to shine Maddie's light. To share the blessing of Maddie. Her story. Her strength. Her inspiration. Her hope. We were blessed to do so not just in a setting saturated with ACS supporters, but one also scattered with family, close friends, current colleagues, former colleagues, and even a handful of special Lurie's Place staff.

I like to think that this speech represented our next forceful steps on the journey through our own personal Hall of Hope. Because that's the hallway we've chosen. Since entering the hospital doors on April 20, 2017, we've always had the opportunity to opt between one of two hallways. A Hall of Despair. And a Hall of Hope. One year later, we're still walking firmly on hopeful ground. Led by the same courageous girl who guided us from the very beginning.

As this year's Lokai Days come to a close, my only prayer is that this hallway is eternal. And that we continue to have the strength to stay within its warm, brightly-lit pathway. With Maddie in our hearts, and Lily by our side, I have no doubt that this prayer will remain our reality.

Thank you as always for continuing to stand beside us on this hope and Maddie-filled walk. Thanks to you, we are not, and have never been, alone on this journey.

Below is the full text of our speech that evening. The theme of the event was "Impacting Cancer from All Angles." Pammy and I were asked to represent the angle of parent and caregiver. We stayed true to the theme in our words. And in honor of Maddie, we executed the speech as intended – as a beautiful, verbal dance. With me and Pammy following Maddie's lead.

SCOTT:

Pammy and I stand before you, proudly, as parents. One year ago, being a parent was everything you would expect for a young couple raising children in our beautiful city. Being a parent meant helping our then two-and-a-half-year-old daughter, Maddie, transition to toddlerhood. Finding her fun activities. Music class. Dance class. Ballet class. Gymnastics class. Swim class. Being a parent meant exploring local parks. Trips to the Shedd Aquarium. Montrose Beach. The Lincoln Park Zoo. The Nature Museum. The Children's Museum. Libraries. Book stores. Play dates. Preschool. Family gatherings. Being a parent meant keeping up with a smiley toddler on the run.

One year ago, being a parent meant preparing for a little sister. As on February 13, 2017, Pammy gave birth to our second child, Lily (otherwise known as Maddie's new toy doll), at Prentice Women's Hospital in the city. Being a parent meant sleepless nights. Endless diaper changes. Washing bottles. Making swaddles. Giggles. Board books. Bibs. Dancing to all things Disney on Pandora.

One year ago, being a parent meant performing the delicate balance of being a good parent and being a good employee. Pammy, as a finance manager at PepsiCo in the West Loop. And me as an attorney at a matrimonial law firm in the city. Being a parent meant leaving for work late enough to grab a quick breakfast with the kids. And coming home early enough for playtime, dinner time, bath time, and bedtime.

Then came April 20, 2017. That night, Maddie and I walked into the Lurie Children's emergency room thinking that she just had a cold. That swollen lymph nodes were causing pain in her neck and discomfort in moving. Maddie arrived that evening with a juice box in one hand and a bag of animal crackers in the other. She left with a diagnosis that would change our lives forever.

As I put Maddie on the scale at triage that night, her legs buckled under her. The same smiley girl who spent her toddlerhood always on the run could no longer bear sufficient weight to stand. As the night wore on, she progressively lost feeling on the left side of her body. Her pain and paralysis worsened. And then just after midnight on April 21, 2017 – exactly one year ago from today – we learned the reason why:

That a rare cancerous tumor was filling four levels of Maddie's little spinal cord. The only path to treatment would require a risky emergency surgery in an attempt to remove the tumor, followed by weeks if not months of physical therapy to try and help Maddie walk again, coupled with a 52-week aggressive chemotherapy protocol, followed by radiation. Each step contingent on Maddie surviving the step before.

Later that morning, Maddie underwent a six-hour emergency surgery to attempt to save her life. As Maddie was wheeled off to the operating room, at that moment, Pammy and I realized we had a choice. A question to answer.

To crumble? Or to care?

To wave the white flag? Or to fight?

PAMMY:

And starting that day, we chose to accept our role of caregiver and fighter with incredible force. To attack cancer with love. With singing. With dancing. With imagination. With care.

Being a parent now meant having the responsibility and the privilege to navigate our Maddie through the darkest waters with the power of love and light.

Being a parent meant me taking a leave of absence from my job at Pepsi to assume the role of captain of the caregiving ship.

Being a parent meant being able to cheer on with pride, as Maddie went from paralysis to miraculous. Emerging from her surgery with minimal physical therapy. And somehow, someway, returning quickly to her dancing, singing, smiling self.

Being a parent meant dancing side by side with Maddie through the crippling side effects of chemotherapy.

Being a parent meant taking a life previously filled with outdoor adventures to bringing the adventure inside our home to avoid risk of infection to her weakened immune system.

Being a parent meant turning hospital stays at Lurie Children's Hospital into "sleepovers." Sleepovers where we ignored the beeping machines and focused on the playroom, on movie nights, and on treasure hunts.

Being a parent meant mentally preparing Maddie for the unimaginable in a way she could understand. Neck braces became necklaces. MRIs became pictures. Doctors became special friends to help the tumor not come back.

And the result was the friendliest, happiest patient dancing her way through the 17th Floor of Lurie Children's Hospital (or as we called it, "Lurie's Place").

SCOTT: But make no mistake, we could not have waged this war of love against cancer alone. Maddie's cancer was attacked from every angle.

PAMMY: By research, that amazingly had advanced enough to provide us with an identifiable protocol to address a cancer affecting only 30-50 kids per year in the U.S.

SCOTT: By access to care, as we were blessed to live in close proximity to one of the greatest children's hospitals in the world.

PAMMY: By child life specialists and social workers, who gave us the tools to talk to Maddie about her cancer and her treatment in a way she could understand.

SCOTT: By employers, who gave us whatever support we needed to maintain our jobs at an unthinkable time.

PAMMY: By quality insurance, that ensured we could fight Maddie's cancer without filing for bankruptcy.

SCOTT: By family and community, who gave us the strength, support, and childcare coverage to always be able to stand by Maddie's side.

PAMMY: By Lily, who gave us the giggles to grit through each day.

SCOTT: By Maddie, who heroically faced her disease with a dance in her step and a smile on her face.

PAMMY: And by incredible charitable organizations, like the American Cancer Society, who work tirelessly to support families like ours. And literally operate as the people on the ground helping to solidify and strengthen each of these many angles.

SCOTT: Ultimately, being a parent during Maddie's battle with cancer will forever be one of the greatest privileges of our lives. But unfortunately, as all too many parents of a child with cancer know, this privilege also can come with unspeakable pain.

That pain came for us on January 4th of this year. When Maddie's battle with cancer ended all too soon. Just after her three-and-a-half-year-old birthday. But I promise you this: although Maddie's battle with cancer may have ended, her war – and our war – is just beginning.

And tonight, each and every one of us has the opportunity to answer the same question Pammy and I asked ourselves exactly one year ago today:

To crumble? Or to care?
To wave the white flag? Or to fight?

While a lot has changed over the course of the past year, our answer has never been stronger. So tonight, let's fight for each and every angle:

Let's fight for the doctors. The nurses. The social workers. The child life specialists. The hospitals.

Let's fight for the researchers. The volunteers. The survivors. The lobbyists. The legislators.

Let's fight for the caregivers. The parents. The grandparents. The sisters. The brothers. The sons. The daughters. The aunts, uncles, and cousins.

And most importantly, let's fight for the patients. The existing patients. The undiagnosed patients. The Maddies of today. And the Maddies of tomorrow.

Tonight, let's give the American Cancer Society the support it needs to attack cancer from every angle. And to one day eliminate this wretched disease from the face of the earth. Thank you all for your support of this incredible organization. And thank you to the American Cancer Society for being the leader in the fight against cancer. We love you, Maddie.

Miracle Update (4/24/18)

Just three days after Discovery Ball, another doorway appeared in our Hall of Hope. We received a message from the Chief Development Officer at Lurie's Place. In a little over a month, the hospital is announcing a new fundraising campaign. The initiative is a $500 million fundraising campaign called "For Every Child." With Lake Michigan providing the inspirational background setting, Lurie's Place will be hosting a beachside kickoff event to announce this major endeavor to three-hundred-plus of its closest charitable-minded friends. Pammy and I have officially been invited to join the evening's speakers and continue to shine Maddie's inspirational light. You know our answer at this point. Because it's not just our answer. It's our duty as Maddie's parents. To keep speaking. To keep inspiring. To keep shining. To keep dancing.

As I relay our immediate affirmative RSVP to this incredible opportunity to create an impact, I hear two voices in my head:

"*Go Go Go!*" screams Lily.

"*Daaaaaadddddyyyyy, coooooome geeeeeet meeeee,*" whispers Maddie.

PART THREE

Miracle Update (4/27/18)

The professional team behind the creation of Dancing While Cancering continues to take shape. After a month-long search, we identified our new accountant for the organization. Her name is Susan Jones. She's been incredibly supportive and responsive since our initial meeting and has even agreed to walk us through all rudimentary aspects of charity-based debits and credits. By all accounts, she appears to be a wonderful personal, a sharp accountant, and a communicative and thoughtful teacher. We are thrilled to have her as part of the team.

In addition, Susan was able to recommend a local attorney who specializes in nonprofit law to help us finalize both the formation of the organization as well as our application for official 501(c)(3) status (*i.e.*, to be an official charitable organization in the eyes of the IRS). Our previous attorney was a friend who graciously assisted us in our first formative steps. But given the level of growth we aspire to achieve as an organization, it made sense to find someone who specializes in this special and unique area of law. With Susan's assistance, we were able to identify that attorney. Her name?

Sally Wagenmaker.

Wagenmaker. Evokes the sound of Wagon Maker. A fitting name for the attorney who is getting Dancing While Cancering off and running. Or shall I say, off and dancing. I can hear Lily yet again. *"Go Go Go,"* yells Lily! And with Sally's lead, that's exactly what we're doing. After just being engaged for only a week, Sally has transformed the legal vision of our charitable formation. Instead of a private foundation, Sally is forming Dancing While Cancering as a public charity. Legal mumbo jumbo aside, the idea is that the charity will be supported primarily by the outside world, by the public and for the public, and the proceeds will go toward a public need and philanthropic endeavor: bringing joy to the inpatient hospital experience for children with cancer.

As a result, the formation entity will be a corporation as opposed to the previously envisioned trust instrument. And as such, we had a few more decisions to make. The first was to confirm a corporate name. After much discussion, we all agreed that the name Dancing While Cancering The Maddie Kramer Foundation might prove a bit too unwieldy to deliver with each speech given, with each check written, etc. And so we broke it down, just a bit, while still preserving both emotionally important aspects of the name. We decided that the formal legal name will be The Maddie Kramer Foundation. Without question, Maddie must be the foundation of the Foundation. However, the organization will have the capability to "do business as" Dancing While Cancering. A beautiful balance for a beautiful dance. For purposes of our logo, we still intend to preserve and portray both aspects of the name:

Dancing While Cancering
The Maddie Kramer Foundation

However, this legal tweak of differentiating between the formal legal name and the "doing business as" name will allow us and our supporters the ease of use of not needing to write out or say out loud the entire seven-word name each and every time the organization is referenced. Either or both names may be used interchangeably.

As a corporation, we also need to decide on the formation date. The birth date of this inspiring entity. As the calendar nears another turn of the page to May, Pammy and I both knew our answer. This special cause deserves a special date. And so on May 4, 2018, Pammy's 36th birthday, we'll be formally welcoming our Maddie-inspired foundation into the world. Maddie and Mommy united again in such a memorable and momentous way.

Miracle Update (4/28/18)

J ust days before we are scheduled to welcome The Maddie Kramer Foundation into the world, a special package arrived at our doorstep today. A proof copy of the paperback version of *Maddie's Miracles*. With its purposeful subtitle: *A Book of Life*. I touch the gentle cover page for the first time. I smell the sweet pages. I turn to the back cover. I've heard that most popular, publicized books contain a back cover with glowing quotes or reviews. Since we're obviously not at that stage at this moment, we instead provided a preview of what's behind these beautiful pages. The back matter reads as follows:

A Book of Love. A Book of Life. A Book of Loving Life.
In Darkness and In Light.

On April 26, 2017, a loving father opened his laptop with the intent of simply keeping his family and friends updated on the condition of his two-and-a-half-year-old daughter, Maddie. Just days prior, Maddie had undergone emergency surgery to remove a rare, cancerous tumor from her spinal cord. Her battle would continue with an aggressive treatment protocol that would have been taxing on even the strongest of adults. With Maddie as the perpetual force of positivity, her father continued to document her miraculous journey.

Factual updates quickly transformed into a series of inspiring and unforgettable vignettes.

Anyone following Maddie's story began to realize that the daily doses of joy she dropped upon her loved ones were not fleeting tales of a fighting toddler. Instead, there was something deeper about Maddie. Something more profound. Something you will discover as you delve into Maddie's story.

That Maddie - with her boundless miracles and incomparable spirit - offers unique insight into tackling any challenge life may bring our way. That Maddie - from the very beginning - was giving us all the gift of this beautiful book of life.

This beautiful book of life. That's all I feel at this moment. I can't even begin to describe the feeling of holding Maddie's inspirational story in my hands. It's almost like Amazon was our technological stork bringing Maddie's story tangibly back to our doorstep. These pages upon pages of love, tears, and miracles are living proof of the full and meaningful life Maddie lived. The bold and beautiful lessons and experiences she bestowed upon all of us. And as I pull this softly-colored story from the Amazon delivery box, I am filled with a mixed pride and joy to know that no matter what our future holds, Maddie's journey is now memorialized forever. Maddie is here with us. Her story lives on. In this beautiful book of life that I now have the blessing to keep by my side, as we continue our inspirational walk together.

Double Chai (5/4/18)

In Hebrew, the word "Chai" – which means "life" – is associated with the number 18. Today is May 4, 2018. And in this 18th year of the millennium, Pammy turns 36 years old. Her "Double Chai" birthday. In many ways, this year's birthday is very much a birthday of two lives. As our former life is now transitioning into this second life.

While certainly this is not the life we chose, or the life we planned, it remains the life we are embracing. This second life – exponentially more challenging yet teeming with meaning – is doubly full of life. The power packed into each step on this journey is absolutely a Double Chai made up of well more than double the inspiration and double the purpose. And as we continue forward with this inspiration and purpose, we do so carrying Maddie's life, and her miraculous memory, alongside our own lives. When Pammy begins this Double Chai Day, she does so literally carrying on two lives.

But the Double in this Double Chai doesn't stop there. On this Double Chai Birthday, we also have another life to celebrate. Because today, the symbol of this second life and this full life is born. Today, we welcome into this inspired new world:

Dancing While Cancering
The Maddie Kramer Foundation

Today, we officially filed the Articles of Incorporation for Maddie's Foundation. A legal symbol of our new miracle. The mission statement of our newborn brainchild is also now the mission statement of our second life: *bringing joy to the inpatient hospital experience for children with cancer.* Our fearless and fun-filled leader for this mission is no doubt watching as we fulfill, hour after hour, her incredible willpower. Although we have four more months to go until we'll be ready to announce this special birth to the world, we can already feel her impact. Her power. Her strength. Her hope. Her motivation. Her life. And today, on this Double Chai Birthday, we celebrate this simultaneous beautiful beginning of life and our inspired continuation of life. Happy Double Chai, Pammy. May your life continue to be filled with life.

The Audience Revisited (5/7/18)

As Pammy's birthday grew closer, I knew that I wanted to do something light to celebrate. We've had more than enough heavy this year for one lifetime. My search for lightness even extended to my greeting card. Year after year, I've always written Pammy pretty emotional, deep notes for her birthday. A natural yet special opportunity to express my gratitude. This year, I felt like we could both use something different.

My greeting card of choice? A picture of a fish on the outside. The inside then says three simple words:

Enjoy this cod.

Pretty good! I'm only ashamed I didn't come up with the phrase. My handwritten note was not much deeper than this comical cod reference. I plainly and simply expressed a hope for a light, fun night out. And the tickets to that light, fun night out rested gently inside the card. Our destination? Since Peppa Pig Live has yet to return to the Chicago Theatre for reasons I'll never understand, I scoured the internet for the next best gift for every yuppie within 50 miles of Chicago's theatre district: tickets to see *Hamilton*.

Pammy's birthday seemed like the perfect night for this musical reprieve. Celebrations and holidays tend to be uniquely raw. I'd imagine that feeling will probably last for a long time, if not the rest of our lives. Moments of celebration and reflections are just inextricably tied to remembering who's physically missing from these life moments. Without question, Maddie's emotional and psychological presence is everlasting. But that doesn't necessarily make special occasions like birthdays any easier.

Our efforts for emotional escape, however, got off to an excellent start. After an amazing dinner within walking distance of the venue, Pammy and I made our way – hand in hand – to the CIBC Theatre in Chicago. With the sun still shining deep into the evening as Spring sprung into full effect, our transformation into birthday imaginative mode was supplemented by our first weeknight without wearing winter coats in months.

As the curtain rose, and as we heard the first beat blast, we were entranced. The lyrics were mind-numbingly dense. The colors were hypnotizing. The musical pace was unstoppable. Our brains were transported well before our A.C. lives or our B.C. lives. Back to the late 1700s. Immersed in the story of an unheralded Founding Father retold with the rapidity of rap and cannonballs of creativity. A heroic tale of an orphan's revolutionary rise. What could go wrong?

Well, any levity of this lighthearted history lesson came to a crashing halt in the second half. Without much in the way of warning, Alexander Hamilton loses his child to a battle. A gun duel to be exact. Rather than just a passing scene, however, the cast pummels us with an outpouring of emotion in a song called *It's Quiet Uptown*. The common refrain of the chorus? The notion that these mourning parents would be "walking through the unimaginable."

Needless to say, the idea that our light birthday night would transform into an emotional exploration of historical examples of coping with the death of a child was about as unimaginable as it gets. But the uncanny commonality of emotions was beyond eerie. I did not just hear every pained lyric. I felt them. Essentially paralyzed by the emotional pain. While still allowing myself to immerse in the meaning just as I have with every other seemingly not so random lyric that has waltzed into our A.C. World. Whether Daniel Tiger, Moana, or Hamilton, there is meaning to be found everywhere. You just need to keep your eyes and ears open.

But walking through the unimaginable of Hamilton's child's death was only the beginning of our unexpected foray into this all too non-fictional show. The conclusion of the performance centered around the randomness of death. And the uncertainty of legacy. In doing so, three lines are repeated perhaps more than any other in the entire show:

Who lives?
Who dies?
Who tells your story?

In the musical and in history, Alexander Hamilton ultimately passes away prematurely. But his wife, Eliza, carries the bright light of his torch only to tell the incredible story of Alexander's life. And in the process, she commits herself to making the world a better place in the precise places that impacted Alexander; namely, becoming the co-founder of the first private orphanage in New York City. As the curtain falls, we're immersed in the impact that Alexander – both individually and through Eliza – left on this world. And the last visual image for every viewer is Eliza's face, as she too makes her way to heaven. Letting out a gasp of amazement, as she makes contact with her beloved while she transitions to the other side.

Who lives?
Who dies?
Who tells your story?

This might not have been the light night of entertainment for Pammy's birthday that we intended to play out. But as with nearly all experiences these days, the show was again filled with Maddie's bright and bold light. In our case, we know the answer to those three questions just as definitively as Eliza. Pammy, Lily, and I are all left to proudly carry that same torch of inspiration and tell Maddie's story. And just months after our first brush with Hamilton's boundless beauty, Maddie's own story will soon be told. From the unimaginable to pure imagination. From paralysis to miraculous. From B.C. to A.C. But in all cases, a story of love. In all cases, a story of life. In all cases, a story of loving life. In darkness and in light.

We love you, Maddie. So long as Mommy, Lily, and I are around, your curtain will continue to rise. Because your story is only just beginning.

Taste of Hope (5/10/18)

A few weeks ago, I was a guest at a networking event hosted by a local steakhouse. The event was attended by thirty or so local professionals, and the primary purpose was simply to meet new people who may share common clientele or interests. With that in mind, I was attending primarily in my capacity as a family law attorney. Events such as these are often a nice way to discover new resources, services, and contacts for my clients (such as trusted financial advisors, insurance brokers, etc.). In order to facilitate that exchange of information, the event's organizer leads an introduction of each professional to the group, as we are all sitting around in a large circle in a banquet space within the restaurant.

Unbeknownst to me, the event's organizer (who I also know on a personal level) had different plans that morning for me. Touched by Maddie's story and our journey, he asked if I would feel comfortable sharing our experience, and the path we're currently walking, with the group. With little time to react, I took the plunge. And tried my best to give these thirty guests a sense of Maddie's inspirational influence and our hope to carry that inspiration forward through our philanthropic endeavors. Despite the unexpected nature of the request, it felt no less beautiful to share Maddie's story.

As has often been the case with all things Maddie, the chance encounters and coincidences followed shortly thereafter. While chit-chatting with guests as the event concluded, a woman named Linda approached me and introduced herself. She expressed her heartfelt condolences and let me know that she was very active within the American Cancer Society. Specifically, she is on the planning committee for a local fundraising event called "Taste of Hope." She explains that the annual event, which is filled with food and wine tastings and appearances from local chefs, has been growing rapidly, and their goal is to become the premier culinary-based fundraising event in Chicago.

During our conversation, I briefly let her know about our support for the American Cancer Society and our various experiences with the organization. Without hesitation, she asks to put me in touch with the lead Society employee for the event with a hope that Pammy and I would attend the next planning committee meeting and share Maddie's story with the group as a source of inspiration for their efforts. Like with all such requests in the past couple of months, I immediately say yes and welcome the opportunity to shine Maddie's light, especially within a group of motivated, cancer charity supporters.

A few days later, Pammy and I receive a formal invitation to attend the committee meeting from the Chicago-based Society employee, Meghan, who coordinates the events. Lo and behold, Meghan (who I had never met previously), attended Discovery Ball the other week. She shared how touched and inspired she was by Maddie's life. She expressed delight at the idea of us continuing to share our journey with her fellow Taste of Hope committee members.

And finally, unexpectedly, she let me know that sitting directly next to her at work at that very moment was her office cubemate.

Who might that be, you ask? None other than my sister, Amy.

Yet again, our walk through this Hall of Hope continues to be filled with chance encounters and coincidences. With that circuitous and unlikely background, Pammy and I joined the professional, kind, and motivated group of Taste of Hope committee members at their planning meeting today. In sharing Maddie's story, we noted how meaningful and powerful their event name felt to us. That me and Pammy very much felt acutely the impact of having a "taste of hope." That the chef for our taste of hope, Maddie, served up more than just a taste over the last year – she was delivering a seemingly endless buffet of hope and inspiration. And that our job, from April 21st onward, has been to keep Maddie's inspiration kitchen cooking. To ensure that January 4th did not take away our flame. To keep serving up ongoing tastes of hope. Spoonful by spoonful. Speech by speech. Meeting by meeting. Donation by donation. Conversation by conversation. Hopeful event by hopeful event.

Thank you, Taste of Hope planning committee, for your generous invitation and warm presence. We wish you a beautiful night of hope during your event this Fall. And appreciate you playing your part in the fight against cancer. We plan to be there by your side that evening. With a spoon in our hands. And Maddie in our hearts.

Miracle Update (5/11/18)

After our inspirational meeting yesterday, Pammy and I delivered another little taste of hope this afternoon. This taste was delivered in an envelope. To the Internal Revenue Service (I know, not the first place your mind goes when you think about hope and inspiration). But yes, on this Friday, May 11, 2018, we submitted our application to be recognized formally by the IRS as a 501(c)(3). Our understanding is that the approval process takes around four months, which places us right around the exact time that we hope to launch Dancing While Cancering (at the conclusion of Childhood Cancer Awareness Month in September).

With our formal legal steps behind us, Pammy and I will now be focusing on two primary developments: a) our website and logo to deliver Maddie's inspirational mission; and b) our welcome bags (which we're now calling "Smile Packs") to deliver a taste of hope – and a taste of Maddie's energetic spirit – to the current and future patients at Lurie's Place and beyond.

Pammy and I are both so filled with Maddie's meaning at this moment. Holding on to Maddie's hope. Ignited by Maddie's inspiration. Cue Lily's motivational mantra: *Go Go Go!*

Graduation Inspiration (5/12/18)

Seven years ago, our family lost another bright light to cancer. My grandmother's sister (and my great aunt), Rosilyn Pomerantz. "Aunt Rozzie" had a smile that could light up a room and an infectious laugh that always left you longing for more. To this day, I can picture her sitting in the front row of our wedding in August 2010. Smiling. Laughing. Spreading her own effervescent light. I vaguely remember hearing at the time that she was having some ongoing pain near her abdomen. A few weeks later she would be diagnosed with late stage pancreatic cancer. And within just a few months, the sound of her laughter quieted. And her smile left this physical world all too soon.

Just like Maddie, however, Aunt Rozzie left a trail of inspiration behind her. In Aunt Rozzie's case, her journey left a particularly striking mark on my sister, Jamie. In 2014, with Aunt Rozzie in her heart, Jamie applied to – and was accepted at – the University of Iowa Nursing School, one of the top undergraduate nursing programs in the country. As early as 2014, what was Jamie's specific desired career path of choice? To become a nurse for pediatric oncology patients.

Jamie, or Aunt Jamie as she is affectionately known in our household, is a light unto her own. With thirteen years separating our respective birthdays (as Jamie likes to say, she was the best idea my mom and dad *never* had), in many ways Jamie was my first child. I still remember her own toddler days. Jamie was like Maddie's spiritual twin. I picture little Jamie toddling around our childhood home. Or more poignantly, I picture little Jamie running around in nothing but her diaper, putting on singing and dancing shows for my easily entertained high school friends. The personalities of Jamie and Maddie were so similar that oftentimes even my visual recollections blur. On many occasions I've even accidentally referred to Maddie as Jamie and vice versa. Whatever differences may exist between Maddie and Jamie, their similar smiles, energy, dance moves, and light, all brought the same sense of hope and love to our family.

And so not surprisingly, from the day Maddie was born, Aunt Jamie and Maddie had a special bond. Whenever Aunt Jamie would come home from college, Maddie would light up immediately. Aunt Jamie was Maddie's aunt, her preschool teacher, her camp counselor, her storyteller, and her choreographer all wrapped up into one. That special role only magnified after April 21st. Without exception, Aunt Jamie brought 110% of her bright light to every visit with Maddie. Aunt Jamie and Maddie would play for hours during our non-hospital stay days of 2017. When those two lights collided, no sunglasses in the world could keep you from being blinded by their brightness. Suppressed immune system and energy be damned, Maddie would play for hours in Aunt Jamie's presence. And Pammy and I (almost replicating precisely my former high school self) would watch in awe and appreciation of each giggle. Each song. Each dance.

Fast forward to today. Filled with pride, I had the privilege of sitting in awe and appreciation of Jamie yet again. Only this time I did so on the University of Iowa campus. As Aunt Jamie graduated at the top of her nursing school class. Unwavering in her commitment to become a pediatric oncology nurse.

Needless to say, none of us could ever foresee the life-altering bookends to Jamie's nursing career. A fourteen-year-old girl driven to study by the darkness of her aunt's disease. A twenty-two-year-old young woman accepting her diploma with her bright and beautiful little niece held in her heart. Despite her young age, Aunt Jamie never let these heartbreaking experiences slow down her inspirational dance. With Aunt Rozzie and Maddie by her side, Aunt Jamie continues her life the same way she started it. The same way Maddie joined it. She keeps dancing along through school. Dancing along through career. Dancing along through life. Only she does so now with generations of inspiration propelling her forward.

Any doubt of Aunt Jamie's inspired drive would be put to rest with a quick glance at her graduation cap. Bedazzled with gold glitter. A picture of Tinkerbell. And an inscription inspirationally lining the remainder of the cap:

All you need is faith, trust, and a little pixie dust.

Congratulations, Aunt Jamie. While I wish I could take away every bit of pain that you've experienced at all-too-young of an age, I am so incredibly proud of the woman you have become. I am fortunate to call you my sister. Maddie was blessed to call you her Aunt. And those other little brave patients out there will be blessed to have such an amazing dance partner by their sides.

Chance Encounters of the Not So Coincidental Kind? (5/13/18)

Since Maddie's journey began, the volume of chance encounters and coincidences have been staggering. Perhaps none greater than the opening chapter of this book, as our three chance encounters with Dr. Erin – diagnosis day, recurrence day, and transition day – loom large over our conception of the meaning of coincidence. Aunt Jamie's graduation brought me front and center with another previously untold story of unparalleled coincidence. A story of Aunt Jamie's first shift during her internship as a pediatric oncology nurse.

In the days preceding Maddie's final sleepover at Lurie's Place, Aunt Jamie had just learned that she secured her top choice of internship. As a senior in the nursing school, you are required to rank your various preferences for nursing internships. Aunt Jamie's top choice was pediatric oncology. As you can imagine, Aunt Jamie never envisioned walking the University of Iowa Stead Family Children's Hospital hallways with personal experience. This was supposed to just be an internship. A preview at a career. Instead, as Aunt Jamie's first evening shift arrived, just days after Maddie's passing, this career preview was also a personal review. Of all the memories of Maddie from her Lurie's Place legacy. Of Maddie shaking her diaper padded rump across the 17th

Floor. Of Maddie meandering her way to her playful playroom retreats. Of Maddie singing. Of Maddie dancing. Of Maddie playing. And certainly, with Maddie's most harrowing days only inches away from Aunt Jamie's mental rearview mirror, the more painful images were appearing even more closely than they were.

With the weight of Maddie's passing on her shoulders and the inspiration of Maddie's life under her feet, Aunt Jamie stepped into the room of her first patient. Her first ever patient in her role as a pediatric oncology nurse. Aunt Jamie had no choice in the patient selection. No role in who she would be first navigating along their cancer journey. And yet who was laying before her in this hospital bed? In a hospital filled with patients across age ranges and diagnoses?

A toddler. With AT/RT. The same very rare cancer that just took her precious niece from this physical world only days before.

Chance encounters and coincidences. I was speechless on hearing the story. After all, there are just 30-50 children per year diagnosed with AT/RT *in the entire country*. Here you have one hospital in the middle of Iowa City, Iowa. Where we have since learned that the only reason they even accepted this unlikely patient was that *one doctor* previously treated *one patient* with AT/RT and so there was sufficient experience to again treat this *one-of-a-kind disease*.

As you can imagine, I was not the only one again questioning the random or not-so-random nature of these experiences in the A.C. World. But as with Dr. Erin, the actual answer to whether this was coincidence or not is irrelevant to me. What matters, and what will continue to drive me, is to derive meaning from our experiences. To take that moment, whether a graceful gift from the powers that be, or a chance encounter filled with all the unlikelihood and randomness that is cancer, and feel the reminder. The reminder of Maddie's journey. The reminder of Maddie's love. The reminder of Maddie's inspiration. The reminder of Maddie's spiritual presence even if her physical body is dancing on another plane. The reminder of why we are walking this walk. Whether that is a reminder of why Aunt Jamie became a nurse, why she should continue to advocate for patients, why Pammy and I are working on writing a book, why we are starting a foundation, or why we are trying to make an impact on the world around us.

Maddie is why. And these chance encounters and coincidences remain our reminder. Our reminder to pause. Our reminder to channel Maddie. Our reminder to keep going. Our reminder of her mindful call: *"Daaaaaaadddddddy, coooooooooome geeeeeeet me…"* We're all coming, kiddo. And we know these reminders of your inspirational spirit will continue to show us the way.

Field of Dreams (5/14/18)

On the way home from Aunt Jamie's graduation, my two other sisters – Jennifer and Amy – and I took a little detour from an otherwise dull highway drive. With some daylight to spare, we decided to go approximately 122 miles out of the way. For a taste of nostalgia and dreams. Driving through endless farmland and cornfields, we landed in the location where many of us learned where heaven really lies…in Dyersville, Iowa. The home of the famous ballfield in the cornfields, the *Field of Dreams*. If you have not seen the movie before, that's a mistake to rectify immediately. Because this is not just a film about baseball. It's a film about dreams. About hopes. About family. And it all takes place in this literal diamond in the rough.

Jennifer, Amy, and I showed up prepared. Each of us wearing a navy shirt with the bright white letters reading:

Is this Heaven?
No…it's Iowa

We took pictures. Smelled the crisp farm air. Filled ourselves with our childhood memories. Stood along the baselines. Looked out at the idyllic family life embodied by the porch swing rocking from the white-picket-fence-enclosed house along the first-base line. And at least in my case, I took a moment to dream again. Just months away from launching a foundation in honor of the most inspirational little girl I've ever met, I took to the base paths. I slowly trotted along from first base. I see the seeds of fertile land beginning to grow in the outfield. I round second, and I think of all the lives we have a chance to fill with joy. I turn the corner for home and thank Maddie for all the beauty she brought our way. I near home plate. With my sisters in the background. Maddie in my heart. Standing in the very place where Ray Kinsella reunited with his father's ghostly spirit on his heavenly field. And I can hear one of the final exchanges from the film, as Ray looks around, hears the sweet sound of his daughter's voice from the porch swing, ponders his life past and life ahead:

Ray: Is there a heaven?
Ray's Father: Oh yeah. It's the place dreams come true.
Ray: Maybe this is heaven.

For all the pain. For all the tears. For all the heartache. I can still feel deeply at this moment for whom we are rounding life's bases. I can still feel deeply our purpose. As I write this chapter, Lily has just woken up from her nap. I see her smiling on the monitor. I hear her chatting away. I make my way upstairs and peek into Maddie's precious, pink room. Her beautiful pictures lining every open space.

We're coming, Maddie. Rounding the bases together. Enveloping ourselves with all the dreams and hopes that we can muster during this lifetime. And looking to greet you with open arms when we eventually take our own walk into those sacred cornfields. With you and Lily as our Miracles and Lights, we are, and will always be, in heaven.

Miracle Update (5/15/18)

As the *Field of Dreams* corn begins to grow, so too do our plans to continue planting the seeds of Maddie's inspirational life story. Over the past couple of weeks, Pammy and I have been discussing ways to spread the love and shine the light of *Maddie's Miracles*. At its core, *Maddie's Miracles* offers inspirational and raw insight into the otherwise dark world of childhood cancer. And so what better time to deliver this story to the world than September 1st – the beginning of Childhood Cancer Awareness Month.

Our goal? To shine Maddie's beautiful and bright light on childhood cancer. To show the world that there is more to walking the cancer walk than the commercials you see on television. To share not just the dark side of childhood cancer. But the inspiration. The strength. The innocence. The life. Because ultimately, Maddie's story is not just one about cancer. It's a story of love. Endurance. Marching forward in the face of the unimaginable. The universal story of grace in the face of grief told through the unlikely heroic eyes of a three-year-old miracle.

And just as with prior steps along our A.C. path, we will not walk this journey alone. Instead, we're turning to our most faithful friends to write this next chapter of awareness during a month of awareness. To Team Maddie. From the grassroots of family and long-time friends, to the broader army of employers, colleagues, Lurie's Place pals, American Cancer Society ambassadors, and all others who supported us along the way. We hope to enlist their help in creating a beautiful, month-long grassroots campaign of love. To bring awareness to childhood cancer in a way that this world has never seen before. And to hopefully transform that awareness into unstoppable action, as *Dancing While Cancering* will thereafter carry Maddie's untamed torch to the cancer dance floor in an effort to bring joy to the other little miracles that follow.

Let's hope the world has a nice big pair of sunglasses ready for September 1st. Because Maddie is coming. Until then, we have some more light to shine this summer. Next up, our June 7th speech to kickoff the new Lurie's Place campaign, "For Every Child." Where the audience is about to hear the story of a very special girl. A special girl who I believe, in my heart of hearts, is just months away from making her everlasting mark on this world.

We're Still Standing (6/3/18)

Today was National Cancer Survivors Day. When I awoke, I couldn't help but recall last year's National Cancer Survivors Day. Maddie and I raced downstairs before the sun came up. Disney Junior was airing a new Doc McStuffins episode – *Hannah the Brave* – in honor of this meaningful day. The episode featured a pediatric cancer patient who always carried a special sidekick named Hannah along her journey. A sidekick who provided her comfort and strength during her time of need. While not exactly *The Shawshank Redemption*, the episode was still a pretty amazing display of light in the face of darkness.

Last year, following up my inspiring morning with Maddie and Doc, I took to my computer (the original blog post is called "I Hope…" and can be found at http://maddiesmiracles.wordpress.com). My fingers guided me through a mental escape filled with hope. Hope for the future. Hope for Maddie's future. Hope for our family's future. National Cancer Survivors Day offered a chance to take a break from our steadfast immersion in the present and instead wander into the promise of a true A.C. World. When the word "patient" would be replaced with "survivor." When dreams could become reality. And my dream was that this annual occasion could become a yearly celebration of overcoming the unfathomable.

One year later, as you can imagine, waking up on National Cancer Survivors Day took on a different feeling. I tried my best to remain hopeful. I took a moment to re-read last year's post. To try and channel the inspiration that Maddie provided that day. Try as I might, the day was a bit of a struggle. Grappling with the reality of National Cancer Survivors Day seemingly not being the day I had so desperately hoped it would be.

But just as the promise of this previously sacred day seemed to be escaping, our own special sidekick decided to write her own narrative. When Lily – who like Hannah the Brave has provided comfort and strength to her parental sidekicks in their time of need – decided to look up at me and Pammy. She gives a smile, as if she knows that she's carrying a special message to deliver. And she lifts herself to stand – without assistance – for the first time in her fifteen-month-old life.

I'm immediately hit with two takeaways. One, it's amazing how a few extra pounds of pudge can delay your movement milestones. But more importantly, Lily reminded us that National Cancer Survivors Day is still a day to cherish. And is still a day for our family to carry with pride. Because in many ways, we are all very much survivors. We are all carrying on Maddie's legacy. We are all carrying on Maddie's message of hope. We are all the ones standing. On Maddie's inspirational shoulders. With Lily willing us forward in this A.C. World with the cutest open-mouthed smile imaginable.

With our incomparable Miracles and Lights behind us, Pammy and I take our next steps into this continued, beautiful hall of hope. In four days, Pammy and I will shine Maddie's light off of the gorgeous shores of Lake Michigan.

The same awe-inspiring view that offered us glimpses of hope on the 17th Floor will now be the backdrop of our next attempt to bring hope to others in the name of love. And in the name of Maddie. Because with Maddie in our hearts, and Lily standing firmly on those inspirational toes, hope always remains standing. Hope always survives. Or as my friend Andy Dufresne once said, "Hope is a good thing. Maybe the best of things. And no good thing ever dies."

And so one year later, on this National Cancer Survivors Day, I will once again wander into a world of hope. I hope that Maddie's story can continue to inspire the world around her. I hope that Pammy and I can continue to muster the strength to share her journey in a way that brings not only inspiration but also motivation to fight this wretched disease. I hope that Dancing While Cancering is able to effectively tackle its mission, and Maddie's mantra, of bringing joy to the inpatient experience for other children who have to face this frightening diagnosis. I hope to continue to find peace not just with all things charity but also in work, in family, and in everyday life. I hope to form an unbreakable bond with my *Go Go Go* sidekick, Lily, as Pammy and I help her navigate what will surely be a unique and special childhood. I hope to continue to dream. To continue to hope. To continue to love. To continue to live. Until one day that life gives way. At a time when I can hopefully say that I have given this life every last drop of inspiration I have within me. At a time when I can hopefully say I lived a life of meaning. At a time when I can hopefully again feel that hug that I miss so deeply today. For what will hopefully be our eternal dance.

I hope.

A Promise for Every Child (6/8/18)

L ast night could not have been more beautiful. The setting, the love, and the gratitude was just flowing in all directions. Pammy and I did our best to shine Maddie's beautiful light, and we could feel her presence every step of the way.

As Lurie kicked off their new fundraising campaign – For Every Child – they announced three promises:

1. The Promise of a Cure
2. The Promise of a Safer Space
3. The Promise of a Healthier Future

Over the course of the evening, they announced each promise separately, which would then be followed by a special presentation and the news of an impactful contribution toward their $500 million goal through 2023. Pammy and I concluded the evening by speaking to The Promise of a Healthier Future. Altogether, as of last night, Lurie's Place has already raised over $200 million. With Maddie's beautiful message, I have no doubt they'll continue the charge toward their ultimate mark.

Below is a full text of our inspired remarks:

SCOTT

Tonight is a night of promise.

I've been thinking a lot about that word in the last couple of weeks:

Promise.

Promise as a verb: To promise. To commit. To pledge. To vow. Promise as a noun: Potential. Hope. A sign of good things to come.

For our family, last year was a life-altering intersection of these two meanings of promise. It all started prior to April 20, 2017. When our lives were filled with promise.

The promise of an imaginative toddler. As our almost two-and-a-half-year-old daughter, Maddie, was everything you could ask for in a child. Sharp as a tack. Cute as a button. Sweet as candy. Maddie loved smiling, singing, dancing, playing, running, jumping, arts and crafting. Without exaggeration, the only challenge of raising Maddie was keeping up with her. Because her mind, her legs, and her mouth never stopped moving. Maddie was like a chatty teenager trapped inside a toddler's body.

The promise of a growing family. As on February 13, 2017, our second daughter, Lily, was born at Prentice Women's Hospital here in the city. Lily was full of love, life, and lots and lots of pudgy rolls. From the beginning, Lily's primary purpose in life was to give you the biggest open mouth smile any time you looked her way.

The promise of a loving life together. Despite me and Pammy being young working professionals with packed schedules, we did everything together. Baby classes. Birthday parties. Play dates. Grocery store runs. Pediatrician appointments. Restaurant trips. It might not have been the most efficient way to live, but Pammy and I didn't know the meaning of divide and conquer. Our promise to our children was united and undivided love.

And then, without warning, the bright light of our family's promise was clouded by an unimaginable darkness. When on April 20, 2017, Maddie and I walked into the Lurie Children's Hospital emergency room. Thinking that she just had a cold. That swollen lymph nodes were causing pain in her neck and difficulty moving. I still remember putting Maddie on the scale at triage that night. We were laughing. Joking. Chit-chatting about how much we thought she would weigh. And how I was sure she would be a little taller because she was such a big girl.

And then it happened.

As Maddie's toes touched the triage scale, her legs buckled under her. Her pain levels escalated rapidly. Within a matter of hours, paralysis overcoming the entire left side of her body began to pummel our promise. And sometime around midnight, on April 21, 2017, a Lurie Children's neurology fellow kneeled down before us in the MRI waiting room. She wrapped her hands around her throat. No words. Just motions.

And as Pammy and I sat motionless, we later learned that these hands represented a rare cancerous tumor that was filling four levels of Maddie's little spinal cord. That the only promise of recovery rested on a risky emergency surgery to remove the tumor, followed by weeks if not months of physical therapy to try and get Maddie to walk again, coupled with an aggressive 52-week chemotherapy regimen. Followed by radiation. Each step contingent upon Maddie surviving the step before it.

As Maddie was wheeled off to the operating room later that morning, our two types of promises collided. And our previous path of parental promise was replaced by a new promise. A commitment. A pledge. A vow.

A promise to love Maddie unconditionally. A promise to give her every last drop of care and support within our bodies. And a promise to always be by her side no matter if, when, or how she emerged from her surgery.

PAMMY

And with our promise, the amazing folks at Lurie Children's Hospital quickly gave us reason to hope again. A promise of a new dawn.

Thanks to Dr. Tord Alden (otherwise known as Superman in our home), a neurosurgeon here at Lurie Children's, Maddie's tumor was removed with the precision of an artist. The promise of a recovery that was expected to require weeks, if not months, of physical therapy to enable Maddie to walk again turned into a medical miracle. In just a matter of weeks, Maddie was back to her smiling, dancing, and laughing self. Her mind, her legs, and her mouth returned to full movement.

Thanks to Dr. Jason Fangusaro, and the oncology team here at Lurie Children's, our family was given the hope – the promise – of a treatment protocol. Maddie's tumor was so rare – as in 30-50 new cases per year rare – most hospitals have never seen, let alone cared for, Maddie's cancer. And yet this incredible staff diagnosed her with incredible speed and moved quickly to place her on a treatment protocol. A protocol that offered us the promise of a continued battle.

Thanks to the Lurie Children's child life specialists – or as we call them, The Fun Team – Maddie continued her battle. But just not with traditional weapons. Maddie battled cancer with dancing. With singing. With iPads. With imaginative play. With the best playroom this side of the Mississippi – the 17th Floor Playroom at Lurie Children's Hospital packed with its very own Maddie-sized Frozen castle. Each hospital visit provided the promise of not just medicine…but of playful outlets.

Thanks to this world-class institution, Scott and I were able to fulfill our promise to Maddie of giving her every ounce of our love. To always be by her side. And to forge a path of promise with the support of the most amazing doctors, nurses, social workers, and child life specialists all by our collective side.

SCOTT

This precious path of promise, this path of hope, lasted eight-and-a-half beautiful months. Eight-and-a-half months with Maddie that would not have been possible without Lurie Children's.

But unfortunately, our two types of promises were destined to collide again. This time on January 4th of this year, when the promise of Maddie's recovery was overcome by the pain of recurrence. As Maddie's battle with cancer ended all too soon. Just after her three-and-a-half-year-old birthday.

But Pammy and I made another promise that day. A promise that cancer can never, and will never, take away from us. A promise to take every pound of pain and pour it into positive purpose. A promise to take every load of love that Maddie gave us and loft it right back into the world. With a new promise. A promise for existing and future patients:

A promise of hope. A promise of care. A promise of a healthier future.

And I promise you this…with your help, that promise is possible. Because right now, just blocks away from here, a medical and scientific army of the best of the best is fighting tirelessly to make that promise a reality. Comforting care, clinical trials, cutting edge research. Our Lurie Leaders have incomparable skills and unparalleled training. They just need the financial weaponry. With our collective support, Lurie Children's will continue to give hope. They will continue to give care. And they will continue to fulfill the promise of a healthier future.

In all my reflections on the word "promise" the last few weeks, I've come to a realization. A realization that this final promise – this promise of a healthier future – is in many ways the ultimate promise. Because it's the promise of promise.

For our family. For your family. For every child.

Daddy Forever (6/17/18)

"Do you have any children, Scott?"

I don't quite think I ever realized how often that question gets asked in ordinary conversation until now. Without fail, not a single week goes by where I don't receive this innocent inquiry from at least 2-3 people with whom I'm meeting for the first time. Fortunately or unfortunately for my polite conversational counterpart, I don't spare them from the truth. Although I've experimented with different deliveries, the substance remains the same. In all instances, I am proudly relaying that I have two daughters. An infant named Lily and our older daughter, Maddie, who is looking down on us from heaven. Not exactly your light social starter.

While this warped speed dive into the depths of our duo of darkness and dedication is an undeniable impediment in certain conversational contexts, I can't quite come to grips with an alternative. Because I do have two daughters. And it wouldn't be fair to Maddie, let alone the blood, sweat, and tears (or related smiles, joy, and inspiration) that continue to carry – day in and day out – in her beautiful honor, to just let her ever-present existence fade into the background of ordinary conversation in the name of efficient chats or social norms. In my world, Maddie is not past tense. Maddie is. And Maddie will continue to be.

Where the conversation goes from there depends on the person. Whether the result is an awkward detour or a hope-filled re-route, I leave feeling like I'm continuing to do Maddie proud. Like I'm continuing to shine her light. That's good enough for this Daddy.

Today, the present tense of my paternity was at a peak. Today was Father's Day. A heavy day to say the least. But Lily didn't allow me to waste any time in a state of wallowing or worrying. Instead, come 6:45 a.m., it was already *Go Go Go*, as we continued our 2018 now official tradition of having breakfast together. Every weekend, you can find me and Lily at our favorite local restaurant, as we dine over an omelette, a croissant, and scores of sugar packets (a.k.a. shakers/musical instruments to be played while we wait for our food). Neither the cuddly company nor the food disappoint.

Equally special, my two present-tense daughters each bestowed their own respective Father's Day presents. Lily's came a little early. Last night, just before Father's Day, as she looked me right in the eye, and said through her vintage Lily smile…

"Daaaaa-dddyyyyyyy!"

After seven months of "Da-Da" (which, let's be honest, at any given moment, could've been referring to me, a dog, a door, or her diaper), Lily transformed her rudimentary reference into that extra dose of daddy love that comes with replacing the humdrum of Da-Da with the sweet melody of Daddy. Yet again, Lily continues to play her part in bringing us smiles when we need them the most.

Our moments to smile did not end there either. Sometime around 1:00 p.m. on Father's Day itself, when our holiday of fathers, family, and festive barbeque was starting to fade into a flow of sadness, there she appeared. Maddie, in all her Dancing While Cancering glory, arrived in my inbox – repackaged and ready for the world – in the form of our latest (and near final) version of the foundation logo. The visual was stunning. After months of idea exchanges, font fixes, and icon adjustments, our amazing graphic designer – Mark – delivered a logo that both shines and dances just like Maddie. Perhaps not so coincidentally, the name of the font that bears our inspirational name – Dancing While Cancering – is called none other than "Because I'm Happy." Its dancing, bubbly letters just ooze with Maddie's love and energy.

Standing next to these joy-filled letters, there's a flowing pediatric cancer ribbon. Doused in a Michigan-like maize color, true both to our alma mater and the color for pediatric cancer awareness – this rallying ribbon bears the heart and soul of our mission. That heart and soul can be found directly in the symbolic heart of this cancer ribbon – where you would typically expect to discover nothing but an empty hole where the ribbon winds around in a loop. Instead, filling the hole in the middle of this cancer symbol is the symbol of our sweet Maddie. A bright pink music note. Bringing color, life, and light to the world of cancer. For those not exactly symbolically inclined, our namesake is made self-evident, as in bright pink letters (Maddie's favorite color, as she would let nearly anyone within a 25-foot radius know on a daily basis), there stands her name, holding up the entire rest of the logo: *The Maddie Kramer Foundation.*

So yes, lest you have any doubts, I still have two beautiful daughters. Both providing the incomparable gifts of love and joy that only the innocence and energy of children can fuel. Lily and Maddie, I love you both in a way that no amount of words or books will ever reflect. Because of you, the ribbon of my life will never have a hole. It is always complete with the bright sounds and colors of your daily miracles and memories wrapped tightly inside.

Miracle Update (6/26/18)

Team Maddie,

What a bright and beautiful birthday for a bright and beautiful girl.

We could not have asked for a more meaningful way to commemorate Maddie's birthday. At 12:30 p.m., Pammy and our immediate family walked into the 17th Floor Playroom at Lurie's Place carrying bags upon bags of cars, trucks, and other modes of transportation for "Maddie's Character Closet." A fitting final addition to the character closet, as Pammy, Lily, and I continue to *Go Go Go* our way through this lap of life's journey.

We also entered the playroom carrying a range of emotions. But as we found ourselves greeted by a roomful of our Lurie's Place family (and by roomful, I literally mean a room filled with the entire spectrum of spectacular hospital staff who helped Maddie and our family during this past year...everyone from the nurses to the child life specialists to her neurosurgeon to her oncology team to the development professionals to the executive leadership), those emotions all transformed into pure, Maddie-filled appreciation. Appreciation for the laughs and smiles in our favorite playroom. Appreciation for the endless singing and dancing down the hallways. Appreciation for all the family – Lurie's Place family, genetic family, and broader Team Maddie family – who made those memories possible. And appreciation for the opportunity to channel that love into this Maddie-inspired creative closet that will bring joy to the other children for years to come.

As it has so many times this past year, Lurie's Place turned an otherwise emotionally challenging day into something special. After touching introductory remarks by Maddie's oncologist (Dr. Jason) as well as our post-January philanthropic partner in crime (Grant Stirling, Lurie's champion of development), Pammy and I proceeded to pass out individual character figurines from Maddie's personal collection to every Lurie's Place attendee. Each character was hand-selected to represent the unique role each Lurie's Place pal played in this past year. As Pammy and I introduced each character, along with the accompanying appreciative explanation, Maddie's love and light filled every inch of empty space in this otherwise packed playroom.

Beaming with Maddie's shining light, Pammy and I then proceeded to formally unveil "Maddie's Character Closet" on behalf of our family and all of Team Maddie.

Thank you all for your special role in our lives. And thank you for making this birthday as unforgettable as the little girl whose incomparable spirit keeps us going on our journey of joy and inspiration.

Happy Birthday, Maddie (6/26/18)

Dear Maddie,

Happy 4th Birthday, sweet girl. We had such a special day thinking about you, kiddo. We went to Lurie's Place with so many of your favorite people. Grandma, Grandpa, Gaga, Pop Pop, your aunts, your uncles, and so many of your Super Doctors. Even Erin and Irene – your favorite nurses – were there! We gave everyone who came today a character from your collection. That way, they could always have something special to look at and to remember you by. And boy did we all remember you today! We made a cool sign called a "plaque" to put on one of the closets in the Lurie's Place Playroom. You'll never guess what we wrote on the plaque…"Maddie's Character Closet!" The closet is so awesome, Maddie. We put all your favorite characters inside. And they each have their own house just for their family. The Tiger family has their own house, Peppa's family has their own house, the Bubble Guppies…everybody! Mommy and I kept saying that if you saw this closet you would just start to smile and laugh because you would love it so much. We thought this closet would be a fun and special way to give other kids at Lurie's Place something awesome to play with. You and your closet are going to make a lot of people smile.

When we were at Lurie's Place, Lily had to stay back home because she was too little to come. But guess who played with her? Your teachers from Gan Shalom, Ms. Marisa and Ms. Brianna! Even Lily's new teacher, Ms. Leah, joined. They had so much fun. You would be so proud of Lily too. She can't walk a lot yet, but she did take three full steps today. On your birthday of all days. And she was playing so fast and fun today. Watching Lily play reminded me a lot of you. She just didn't want to stop! Lily loves you so much, Maddie. Daddy and Lily go into your room every morning to say hi to you. We read your favorite books, we look at pictures of you, and we always tell you how much we love you and miss you.

I'm missing you a lot today, sweet girl. But at the same time, I feel like you are oh so very close to me. Especially when we are at Lurie's Place. Or doing something that helps other people smile. Mommy, Daddy, and Lily are going to keep trying to do special things to make other people smile. In August, right around the day when Mommy and Daddy got married, we are going to share a story about you with the rest of the world. We just know the story is going to make a lot of people smile. Because they are going to have the chance to meet you and read about all the amazing things you did.

After we share your book with everyone, we are going to start a new adventure. We know how much you loved adventures. This one is sort of like our other adventures only we hope this one never ends. It's called *Dancing While Cancering*. On this adventure, we are going to make all the kids at Lurie's Place, and all the other kids who need to take chemo, smile as much as possible. When we first start our adventure, we are going to give them a backpack that has all the fun things you liked to do at Lurie's Place – a speaker to listen to music, instruments to make music, and decorations to make the room look so pretty and fun with lots of colors. It's going to be awesome.

We love you, Maddie. We are just so very proud of you. And we know you are only going to keep making other people happy. Because that's what you do.

Happy birthday, sweet girl.

Love,

Daddy

Miracle Update (7/8/18)

Exactly one month from today, we are set to announce the release of *Maddie's Miracles*. After quietly publishing the book on August 1st, our eighth wedding anniversary, we will share the news with our family and friends starting August 8th. In those seven interim days, Pammy and I just hope to pause. And soak in every ounce of the love and inspiration packed into the beautiful pages of Maddie's story.

A few people have asked me along the way about securing a publisher. While that moment may arrive, we wish to start our journey on a more personal note. Pammy and I both agreed that – at least for purposes of introducing Maddie's story to the world – we want the initial delivery to come from the same people who made this love-filled journey possible. From Team Maddie. With that in mind, we will be self-publishing on Amazon.com. In lieu of any formal marketing strategy, we plan to then share her story with nothing more than the help of Maddie's incredible team. In that way, the beginning of this journey will maintain the touch of intimacy that made Maddie's journey so special. Maddie's story will be brought to life by the same people to whom she brought life: Daddy, Mommy, Lily, and Team Maddie.

As we stand just a month from this literary re-birth, I can just feel Maddie filling my soul. For the past six months, after taking my nightly evening moment to sing goodnight songs to Maddie in her beautiful pink room, I have spent nearly every night reading and re-reading *Maddie's Miracles*. And without fail, every word brings me closer to her. Keeping our spiritual connection strong. Holding on to all the love, smiles, and meaning she gifted to us. This next hallway on our journey through this Hall of Hope is now within sight. My reading and re-reading is about to turn to sharing and re-sharing. Gifting and re-gifting. Inspiring and re-inspiring. I have no doubt that we are going to shine Maddie's unparalleled light upon childhood cancer. To bring light to the darkness. To bring love to the battle. To bring dancing to cancering. We love you, sweet girl.

Walk On (7/26/18)

"Even though I walk through the valley of the shadow of death, I will fear no evil…"

In the days following Maddie's funeral, our Rabbi mentioned how – in the face of death – different mourners focus on different words of this oft-quoted biblical phrase. Some drown in "death." Others emphasize "evil." But in her spiritual wisdom, she encouraged us to focus on a different word. A word so gentle that it is easily lost in the weight of the remainder of the phrase.

Walk.

Despite our Rabbi's advice, Pammy and I probably have not been the best followers. Because starting somewhere around the first step of our Maddie-navigated journey, we haven't done much walking…we ran. All out, non-stop, no-holds-barred, running. Delivering speeches at major events. Fundraising. Forming a nonprofit. Writing a book. Creating a character closet. Raising a one-year-old. Working our respective jobs. Honoring Maddie. Step by step. Mile by mile. Sprint by sprint. Go Go Go.

While our speedy and loving trek has filled our hearts swiftly and soundly, every now and then, we all still need to just walk. To breathe. To slowly soak in our surroundings instead of sprinting for serenity. Tonight, one month after Maddie's fourth birthday, we took a moment to do just that. The occasion? The 16th Annual "Run for Gus," a Lurie's Place sponsored walk/run (yes, in a rare change of pace, we chose walk), the proceeds of which go exclusively to fund brain tumor research at the hospital.

Pammy and I walked side by side with The Sisters (Aunts Amy, Jennifer, and Jamie) and joined the hundreds of other survivors, mourners, parents, siblings, doctors, nurses, and supporters on a beautiful, warm, breezy evening on a lakefront pathway in Lincoln Park. Without question, if Maddie could have picked a location for a walk (other than perhaps Daniel Tiger's Neighborhood), this would have been the one. Across from her beloved nature museum. Blocks from the Lincoln Park Zoo and her animal friends. Enveloped by aged and beautiful trees. Quite a way to honor our hero.

And at the same time, we couldn't have experienced a better time in life to walk. After sprinting through our post-January 4th life, in less than one week, we will be stepping onto an entirely new road. As we officially welcome *Maddie's Miracles* into the world. And shine her bright light on anyone open to soaking in her endless inspiration. While I am guessing this new road will offer plenty of running lanes, we were reminded today of the importance of just taking a moment to walk.

Even more exciting, we apparently will also have someone else walking by our side for these mindful moments. That's right, just days away from releasing a story of the toddler whose first post-surgical steps lifted our hearts, Lily Bug is now starting to walk without assistance. I can't imagine a more perfect walking partner. Lighting up our path ahead with her own miraculous smiles. Walk on, Lily. We will be right there with you. Every step of the way.

Miracle Update (8/1/18)

Today is the eighth anniversary of our wedding. I set my alarm for 4:30 a.m. this morning. I woke up on my own, without the alarm, at 4:25 a.m. I turned off the alarm setting. Took a deep breath. Made my way over to Maddie's room. Sat in her soft rocking chair. The same chair in which we spent so many nights singing "one more song." I opened up the manuscript for *Maddie's Miracles*. After months and months of reviewing and perfecting, all in hopes of being ready to publish on our anniversary, I only made one change. The dedication page, which previously dedicated the book "To Maddie and Lily, our original Miracles and Lights," needed one anniversary update:

And to Pammy, the heart and soul behind Team Maddie.

With that timely and heartfelt addition, I took my second deep breath of the morning. And I clicked "Publish Now" on Amazon's self-publishing website. Nothing to do at this point except wait. And assuming everything goes smoothly, I hope to announce and share Maddie's story with our family, friends, and ever-growing Team Maddie on August 8th. Until then, here's to a meaningful and Maddie-filled week.

<u>Deja Vu (8/7/18)</u>

For weeks now, Pammy and I have set our sights on August 8th as the day upon which we would announce the publication of Maddie's story. Yet here I am, on August 7th, at 11:20 p.m. Just hours away from sharing our meaningful news. And I sit here typing in the very same place that this journey began.

From a Lurie's Place guest bed.

You read that correctly. In an initially frightening (but now calmer) twist of fate, Lily ended up in the Emergency Room tonight after experiencing labored breathing. Thankfully, the doctors quickly concluded that she just has a virus. Bronchiolitis. A condition that manifests itself as a passing cold in most adults. But younger children can experience heightened symptoms. Although Lily's breathing steadied as the night wore on, the doctors agreed we should spend the night as a precaution. Another sleepover at Lurie's Place. Despite the initial concerns, once hearing the diagnosis, Pammy and I released a collective exhale. Needless to say, we can handle Bronchiolitis.

Equally amazing, on this oddly-timed hospital stay, Maddie could not have been more present. With Maddie's

Book of Life just hours away from delivery, we entered an Emergency Room with a room number that has never graced our previous stays: 18. For those keeping score at home, in Jewish culture, the number 18 is the symbol for one everlasting concept:

Life.

As we step into this life-filled room, the movie *Sing!* (one of Maddie's favorites) is already playing on the television. An hour later, *Finding Dory* (Maddie's other Lurie's Place go-to) comes on. Lily points to the screen and says, "Swim swim." Her baby babble attempt to show off her oft-rehearsed Dory/Maddie mantra: Just keep swimming. With I.V. fluids normalizing her heart rate, Lily is greeting nurse after nurse and doctor after doctor with her patented open-mouth smile and a gentle wave of her hand.

A few hours later, we're admitted for an inpatient stay. Hopefully just another night of monitoring before going back home. But for now, I'm awake. All too familiar beeping noises. All too familiar guest bed. My tired fingers typing away as this new journey begins in the same place as it started.

From the beginning, I've struggled to find a place for coincidence vs. fate. The ever-present question of whether any steps along this journey have happened for a reason. As I've said before, it's a tough pill to swallow. The notion that any child would endure disease or distress for a reason would never fully resonate with me. But as always, that is not going to stop me from drawing meaning from the coincidences and miracles that follow. And tonight, on the eve of her literary resurrection, I like to think that Maddie just wanted to say hello. To bring Daddy and Mommy back to Lurie's Place. To show Lily the hallways she has never toddled before (and hopefully will never see again). To begin Maddie's next journey in the same place as her original journey began.

Coincidence or fate aside, I feel your presence, Maddie. I know that you are here keeping Lily safe. Watching over a peaceful sleepover at Lurie's Place. And awaiting your special news tomorrow.

Post-Script (prepared on August 8, 2018):

As if there were any lingering doubts regarding the meaning surrounding the timing of this unexpected Lurie's Place stay, that all dissipated on the morning of August 8th. Lily woke up beautifully. Discharged right before lunch, she was back to her healthy, happy, smiling self. A blip on the radar of life. And yet in these few hospital hours before discharge, I took a brief walk downstairs to say hello to my dad and sister, who were just dropping by to check in.

On this one seemingly fateful walk, maybe a two-minute journey from our inpatient room, I ran into doctor-after-doctor and nurse-after-nurse who had touched our lives during Maddie's lifetime. Starting with the cardiologist who performed Maddie's in-utero echocardiogram while Pammy was pregnant, to the surgeon who installed Maddie's central line, to various nurses and child life specialists who blessed our lives. It felt like an out-of-body, surreal greeting line of gratitude. An unexpected, inexplicable opportunity to thank these special individuals for their special role in Maddie's life just hours before our ultimate showing of gratitude for Maddie is set to be released.

Above all, Lily quickly returned to 100%. A brief moment of darkness in Room 18. Followed by the light. Sounds like a familiar theme. Perhaps more than ever, I enter this moment of shining Maddie's light filled with meaning and gratitude.

Labor of Love (8/8/18 at 1:34 p.m.)

On August 1st, Pammy and I celebrated our 8th wedding anniversary. 8 years might not seem like much. But Pammy and I have experienced a lifetime of ups in downs in those 8 years. Beginning our 8th year of marriage, we can't help but also realize that the number 8 has played an especially prominent, deep, and meaningful role in our lives in the past year. Most poignantly, Pammy and I now enter our 8th month since our sweet Maddie began dancing in heaven. And as we take those next meaningful steps forward, we will forever remember the steady flow of miracles that Maddie's 8-month battle with cancer delivered. Miracles that have been memorialized in these pages and pages of blog posts.

Maddie's Miracles (both in life and online) began with her miraculous recovery from an emergency surgery to remove a rare tumor from her spinal cord in April 2017. Post-surgery, Maddie arrived at the Shirley Ryan AbilityLab entirely unable to walk. Essentially paralyzed on the left side of her body on account of the rapidly growing tumor and her invasive, risky surgery. We were told to expect months of inpatient physical rehabilitation without any guarantee as to her future physical abilities.

Yet despite the challenging prognosis, and with Team Maddie standing firmly by our side, we were blessed with one of many miracles. After spending a mere 8 nights inpatient, Maddie was released to go home. Yes, home. On her own two walking/dancing feet nonetheless. A moment we'll never forget for the rest of our lives. In just 8 incredible nights, Maddie went from paralysis to miraculous. Setting the stage for her 8-month dance through life that we all were blessed to witness unfold.

With Maddie in our hearts, as Pammy and I reflect on our 8 years together, the range of emotions is almost unthinkable. But for all the ups and downs this last year has brought, there was one constant. The same constant that has carried Pammy and me through our 8 years of marriage.

Love.

Unending, unwavering love. Love for Maddie. Love for Lily. And love for one another. With our hearts as full as ever, on this 8th day of the 8th month of the year, it is with unparalleled love that we announce a special labor of love. In memory of our heroic Maddie, we have self-published a book – now available on Amazon.com – bearing her inspirational namesake:

Maddie's Miracles: A Book of Life

This 8-part story contains all the love, beauty, and inspiration that Maddie gifted the world around her. For those who have followed Maddie's journey since the beginning, or for those who are just getting to know her, I promise you this: Maddie has so much light remaining to shine upon this world. And her life's story, told in these inspirational pages, will forever lift up those with the strength and desire to immerse themselves in her powerful message. A message for anyone who has dealt with struggle of any kind. A message for anyone in search of inspiration. A message of love. A message of life. A message of loving life. In darkness and in light.

In sharing Maddie's inspirational message, we are also reminded that September marks the beginning of Childhood Cancer Awareness Month. A month dedicated to raising awareness about the heroic children, families, and friends that are tasked with battling this wretched disease. As a result, we will be donating 100% of our net sales proceeds during Childhood Cancer Awareness Month to cancer charities. In doing so, we also hope to give back to many of the organizations that helped our family along the way.

Moreover, as our inspirational hero taught us, being aware of childhood cancer goes beyond just being aware of the disease itself. Maddie showed us the light, the love, and the heroism that accompanies this otherwise unwanted battle. And so in memory of Maddie, and in honor of the other brave families, friends, doctors, nurses, patients, and survivors out there who have been touched by cancer, Pammy and I invite you to join our campaign to spread awareness of Maddie's story and to *Shine Maddie's Light on Childhood Cancer.*

For 30 straight days, from September 1st to September 30th, Pammy and I will be posting on social media a new inspirational message that we learned from Maddie's journey (and including a link to the book with each post). The format for those messages will be as follows:

Thank you, Maddie, for teaching me [INSERT LESSON].

#ShineMaddiesLight
#MaddiesMiracles
#TeamMaddie

Starting September 1st, we invite each and every one of you to join us in *Shining Maddie's Light* using the same format above. We welcome you to create your own posts, share your own lessons, and/or share those that Pammy or I post. In whatever way you may wish to participate (via social media, e-mail, or in-person conversations), we welcome all the electricity we can muster to shine Maddie's bright light.

Between now and September 1st, feel free to share this message with others. To build up the strength of our already unbeatable team. To raise money for cancer charities. And to get us all geared up for an impactful September.

We have no doubt that Team Maddie is about to light up the world. And that the inspiration Maddie began delivering to us more than one year ago will continue for a lifetime.

Team Maddie Forever.

Miracle Update (8/10/18)

To our ever-growing Team Maddie,

If there were any doubts as to the electricity that Team Maddie was capable of creating, those were put to rest over the last twenty-four hours. Thank you all for your beautiful and inspirational support as we begin this next journey together. We are so grateful for you, and we look forward to continuing to Shine Maddie's Light together.

Miracle Update (8/30/18)

I arrived home today from work around 6:00 p.m. Now just under thirty-six hours from the first post of our #ShineMaddiesLight campaign. Opening our home address mailbox, I notice a letter from the Internal Revenue Service addressed to "The Maddie Kramer Foundation." I freeze. I smile. I open the letter.

Dear Applicant:

We're pleased to tell you we determined you're exempt from federal income tax under Internal Revenue Code (IRS) Section 501(c)(3)…

That's right. Days before Shining Maddie's Light. Exactly one month until we publicly announce Dancing While Cancering. And we receive confirmation from the IRS that Maddie's foundation is now officially a 501(c)(3) nonprofit. Quite a way to go into our campaign to share Maddie's inspiration with the world. We love you, kiddo. Looking forward to a special month ahead.

Starting a Movement (8/31/18)

Movement has played a memorable role in our lives. In Maddie's case, she never stopped moving. Literally. Her mind, her legs, her mouth…Maddie was always on the go. And keeping up with her (both physically and mentally) was the most exhilarating part of knowing Maddie. From the moment she was born, Maddie kept us going. That was never more apparent than during her battle with cancer. Anyone who had the blessing of watching her ever-dancing legs shimmy their way through the unimaginable was lifted to the highest levels of awe and gratitude. Her movement was miraculous.

Lily too has motivated through movement. Well, perhaps not physical movement. After eighteen months of gravity and the laws of baby roll physics holding her down, Lily is finally taking her first toddling steps. But lest you think Lily is comforted by complacency, know that her mental state is immersed in movement. In fact, Lily's first words appeared in the following order:

1) "Da-da" (thanks again, Lily!)
2) "Ma-ma"
3) *"Go Go Go!"*

That's right. Go Go Go. If at any point Lily's playtime pal of the moment isn't fully entertaining her, or if the surroundings of her existing environment aren't satisfying enough, Lily will point to the nearest door and yell, "*Go Go Go!*" Despite her physical restraints, Lily is a girl on the go.

Since January, Go Go Go has been more than an adorable baby trick (although I do laugh out loud every time she says it). Go Go Go has been the personal rallying cry for me and Pammy. Since January 4th, the day our dancing and moving miracle began her angelic dance, Pammy and I have followed Lily's lead. And we have been Go Go Go-ing the hardest and strongest that our minds and bodies can tolerate. We have been Go Go Go-ing for Maddie. We have been Go Go Go-ing for Lily. We have been Go Go Go-ing for each other. We have been Go Go Go-ing for Cancer Awareness. We have been Go Go Go-ing for every other family out there who has to endure this unthinkable journey.

And in just 48 hours, with the first day of Childhood Cancer Awareness Month on the horizon, with Team Maddie by our sides, and with our two mentors of movement leading us forward, together we start a movement. A movement of love. A movement of light. A movement of life.

The battle cry for this movement?

Shine Maddie's Light.

For thirty consecutive days, we will be posting on social media a different and new inspirational message that Maddie gifted us during her journey. Remember, the formula for our movement is as follows:

Thank you, Maddie, for teaching me [insert lesson].

#ShineMaddiesLight
#MaddiesMiracles
#Team Maddie

Within each post, please note we will also share the link to Maddie's inspirational book. 100% of our net proceeds during this Childhood Cancer Awareness Month will go to cancer charities, including the many who have graced our lives during this journey.

We ask you – please join us in our movement to Shine Maddie's Light.

Shine Maddie's Light through creating your own posts. Shine Maddie's Light by sharing/re-posting/re-tweeting our posts. Shine Maddie's Light by sharing copies of her book with others – with friends, with colleagues, with neighbors, with family, with patients, with clients, with clergy, with students, with those in need of change, and with those in a position to effect change, with those in need of inspiration, and with those in a position to spread inspiration. Shine Maddie's Light in your conversations. In your donations. In your actions. In your philanthropic traction.

Our hope is that through our collective electricity, we are going to light up the social media world with one of the brightest lights ever seen. And that when Maddie's bright light is beaming through our shared messages of love and gratitude, the darkness of cancer will be but a blip on the radar. Instead, we'll raise awareness for the strength, the heroism, the inspiration, and the love that carries the families who have to move through this immovable disease. To remind us all why our work here is not done. That the other Maddies of the world, and the other Kramers of the world, need our help. Not just because of the darkness of cancer. But because of the brightness of their light.

We are but a mirror reflecting back the light that this otherwise dark world of cancer needs so desperately. And with your help, during our month-long social media driven movement, I have no doubt that light will be bold and beautiful.

Thank you all for your incredible and moving support. We are forever moved. And in just two days, we move as one.

Go Go Go!

PART FOUR

#ShineMaddiesLight: Day 1 of 30 (9/1/18)

Thank you, Maddie, for teaching me that miracles do happen.

Maddie's first miracle? Going from paralysis to miraculous, as she stood on her own two feet (with a little help from Grandma's iPad) within six days after undergoing a six-hour emergency surgery to remove a rare, cancerous tumor from her spinal cord. Pammy and I are forever grateful for Lurie Children's Hospital of Chicago and Shirley Ryan AbilityLab for making this miracle possible.

(Note: The above excerpt was my first of 30 consecutive social media posts reflecting our commitment to "Shine Maddie's Light" on childhood cancer. Posted every morning for every day of September, each original post also contained what became our signature hashtag (#ShineMaddiesLight) as well as a link to a corresponding chapter from *Maddie's Miracles* that expounded upon the inspirational lesson behind that day's message. For ease of reading, I have not included the hashtag or chapter recitations, but they can be found on our Maddie's Miracles blog at http://maddiesmiracles.wordpress.com.

In many ways, these 30 posts serve as a sweet synopsis of the beautiful lessons that Maddie left the world around her. A summary of her legacy of love. A summary of the miracles that follow. Since Maddie's passing, Pammy and I have held firmly the notion that Maddie's story is not one of cancer. Or death. But one of life, love, and light. These 30 days – immersed in the legacy of life, love, and light that Maddie left behind – will forever remind us of that reality.)

Evening Reflections (9/1/18)

Team Maddie,

Pammy and I could not be more touched by this first day's collective shining. The beautiful pictures. The inspirational messages. The reviews. The shares. The likes. The love. The light.

Together, we embodied the inspirational energy bottled by our little bundle of love and light. As one special Team Maddie member said today, "Put on your sunglasses and get ready for the impact Maddie will continue to make." We couldn't agree more. Team Maddie could not have shined more brightly or beautifully. Watch out, Cancer. We're coming for you…

(Note: What you will not find in the pages that follow is the endless flow of text messages, e-mails, phone calls, social media comments, and other Maddie-fueled love that Pammy and I received after each morning's post. Collectively, the other-worldly support stood as an unparalleled illustration that the worst in life can bring out the best in humanity. Buoyed by the love and support from our family, friends, and growing Team Maddie, I found myself unexpectedly inspired each evening to reflect on the morning's post in some capacity. These "Evening Reflections" were entirely unplanned. While the context for certain reflections may be difficult to convey without the underlying social media post, the impact of each day's inspiration is palpable. At the very least, these Evening Reflections will forever offer a window into the blinding light that Team Maddie shined for 30 incredible days of awareness and love. Powered by the most heroic little girl that I will ever have the privilege to know.)

#ShineMaddiesLight: Day 2 of 30 (9/2/18)

Thank you, Maddie, for teaching me the magic of an uneventful day.

After ten straight days filled with everything from trauma to terror to challenge to gratitude to elation, I'll never forget Maddie's first uneventful day post-surgery at Shirley Ryan AbilityLab. This much needed ordinary evening concluded with a volunteer magician who, supported by Maddie's special powers, reminded us about the magic of an uneventful day.

Evening Reflections (9/2/18)

Team Maddie,

Tonight, Pammy and I took a moment to have a belated anniversary celebration. The first time we've been out together for a nice dinner alone in a very long time. As the evening came to a close, the waiter started to describe one of the dessert options. He's walking us through some wild dish that literally involves a tableside flame and chocolate sauce, and he says the following:

"And what better way to put out a fire than with some chocolate?"

Little did he know, we couldn't have agreed more. Putting out fire with chocolate. Maddie and Lily have been helping us do that for more than 19 months straight now. And to Team Maddie, thank you for all the sweet symbolic social media chocolate you've been delivering on Day 2 of #ShineMaddiesLight. Keep shining. Keep spreading the sweet. Keep sharing. Keep reviewing. Keep reading. Keep posting. Keep liking. Keep loving.

We love you. And despite the theme of my #ShineMaddiesLight post today, there was nothing uneventful about this magical day.

#ShineMaddiesLight: Day 3 of 30 (9/3/18)

Thank you, Maddie, for teaching me the power of living in the present.

Following twelve straight days of sleeping in a strange hospital bed, fresh off an unthinkably traumatic experience, what were Maddie's first words after awaking from a full night's sleep? "Daddy, we need to go to the store and get a Grandpere!" (For those not on top of their *Daniel Tiger's Neighborhood* game, Grandpere is Daniel's French-speaking grandfather…and he happened to be one of the few plush characters that Maddie had yet to receive as a gift as of her second week of post-surgery life.)

Evening Reflections (9/3/18)

Team Maddie,

As the first three days of our Labor of Love during this Labor Day weekend come to a close, Pammy and I noticed something special about Maddie's picture in this morning's post. There are three main visuals in the picture: Maddie; a helping hand; and an electrical outlet.

How fitting. Because all three of those visuals have combined for an overwhelmingly inspirational kickoff to our #ShineMaddiesLight campaign. With your helping hands, we have created an electric storm of light and love. All powered by the electrical force that is Maddie. Thanks to you, Maddie's light could not be shining brighter.

Although Labor Day weekend is almost over, our Labor of Love continues. Whether you have known Maddie since birth, or you are just reading about her for the first time in this post, everyone is welcome aboard this solar-powered love train.

Remember, a simple "Share" can create a complex wave of light. A brief post can coax a long-lasting smile. A little girl, full of love, can create a lifetime of inspiration.

#ShineMaddiesLight: Day 4 of 30 (9/4/18)

Thank you, Maddie, for teaching me what it really means to turn raindrops into lemon drops and gum drops…and for dropping daily doses of joy on all of us who were blessed to endure the storm by your side.

Evening Reflections (9/4/18)

Team Maddie,

There is one quote from *Maddie's Miracles* that I keep revisiting today:

I know this is only the beginning, Maddie. But I couldn't be prouder of you. You are the sunshine that follows the rain. You are the light that leads us through the darkness. You are our umbrella. And we love you.

This chapter was written sixteen months ago to the day. And yet, despite all that has transpired since, every single word remains just as true today as it did on May 4, 2017.

Thank you, Team Maddie, for continuing to keep Maddie's light shining. This is only the beginning. Together we have so many more of Maddie's lemon drops and gum drops to share with the world.

#ShineMaddiesLight: Day 5 of 30 (9/5/18)

Thank you, Maddie, for teaching me to take a moment. First thing each morning. To pause. Quiet my mind. Restart. And absorb gratitude.

Evening Reflections (9/5/18)

The chapter included in today's excerpt from *Maddie's Miracles* shared the power of four simple words:

"Daaaaadddy...come geeeeeet meeeeee."

Ever since January 4th, I still wake up to the same morning routine. I pause. Quiet my mind. Restart. And absorb gratitude while hearing Maddie's sweet voice playing in my head:

"Daaaaadddy…come geeeeeet meeeeee."

Because in my mind, I am still striving to come get Maddie every morning. Only now I strive to come get Maddie through my actions in the day ahead. I strive to come get Maddie through my approach to life. I strive to come get Maddie through shining her beautiful light.

So tomorrow, when you wake up, give this a try. Pause briefly. Quiet your mind. Restart. And as you fire up your Facebook account, channel the inspirational message that speaks to you loudest. And share our #ShineMaddiesLight post to shine yourself.

We're all coming for you, kiddo. One beautiful post at a time.

#ShineMaddiesLight: Day 6 of 30 (9/6/18)

Thank you, Maddie, for teaching me that pain and faith can co-exist. Because as tempting as it might have been to curse for the curses, you made sure that I never lost sight of feeling grateful for the goodness.

Evening Reflections (9/6/18)

Grateful for the Goodness.

It's a nice mantra to say the least.

No sooner did I submit this morning's post than did I encounter my first splash of gratitude. Our Guru of Goodness, Lily Bug (that's Maddie's little sister for those new to the journey), was ready to go this morning. When I walked into Lily's room to say good morning, this Goodness followed (as a preliminary translation, note that when Lily says "Hug-a-You," that translates in adult language to "will give me a hug"):

Lily yells, verbatim, with a huge smile on her face, "Da-ddy, Hug-a-You! Mo-mmy, Hug-a-You! Pop Pop, Hug-a-You! Gaga, Hug-a-You! Sue Sue (Lily's nickname for Grandma Sue), Hug-a-You! Bop-ba (Lily's attempt at Grandpa), Hug-a-You…"

And so it went. For about two straight minutes, as Lily rattled off every family member or close friend who she was hoping would give her a hug that day. Or shall I say, who would "Hug-a-You!"

With Lily keeping us smiling, and Team Maddie propelling us forward, there is no shortage of Goodness. Thank you all for continuing to share Maddie's story and shine her beautiful light. Our collective Goodness is making its way across households everywhere. I look forward to seeing so many of you in person. So I can express my gratitude live for all of your Goodness. And to Hug-a-You!

#ShineMaddiesLight: Day 7 of 30 (9/7/18)

Thank you, Maddie, for teaching me that there's a difference between living in the moment and living in the minutia of every minute.

Understanding that distinction was never more critical than when Maddie's 52-week chemotherapy protocol began (yes, for those new to Maddie's journey, you read that correctly – 52 weeks). As challenging as that mindset adjustment might seem given the circumstances, per usual, Maddie made the transition effortless. Living in the moment was the only way of life she knew. And so in every which way, from the first minute of Maddie's treatment, she was showing us the way forward.

Evening Reflections (9/7/18)

Moments vs. Minutia.

One thing is for sure even after today's post – there is not an ounce of minutia in these Maddie-filled moments filling our social media timelines. The content of our posts, and this collective display of love and light, is the essence of what life is all about. Moments like this month do not come often:

Moments to bring light where there is otherwise darkness.

Together we are shining that light brighter every day. Directing Maddie's warm rays to a new person who accesses their phone or computer only to be unexpectedly greeted by a shining share, a fiery forward, or a ray-filled retweet.

Keep Shining. Keep Sharing. This is our Moment!

#ShineMaddiesLight: Day 8 of 30 (9/8/18)

Thank you, Maddie, for teaching me that every day may not be good, but there is good in every day. And for us, there was never really much doubt as to who would be delivering that goodness.

Evening Reflections (9/8/18)

Team Maddie,

Thank you for another bright day of #ShineMaddiesLight. Your likes, your shares, and your light all ensure that there is good in every day.

Because of you, not a day goes by where I'm not receiving a message from at least one new person who is inspired by Maddie's story. Just think, today at least 25 people shared this morning's post – that's at a minimum 10,000 new people receiving good in their day. In the case of #ShineMaddiesLight, sharing really is caring!

As we continue to #ShineMaddiesLight, you never know what particular message will bring good to someone's day. So please don't feel limited to sharing my posts. Whether you've met the posting friend before or not, we are all Team Maddie. And we all have the same goal – shining light. Please instead share any post that inspires you. Whether from me, a friend, a relative, or a complete stranger. Because you never know which of your friends may be in need of good in their day…and whose post might prompt it.

At the very least, if we can keep this Maddie-filled inspiration flowing, there will be so much more good in all of our days.

#ShineMaddiesLight: Day 9 of 30 (9/9/18)

Thank you, Maddie, for teaching me that we are all writing our own Book of Life. And no matter how difficult any particular chapter might be, we can't just live for turning the page. We instead must live for each word. Each splash of symbolism. Each drop of meaning.

To those celebrating Rosh Hashanah today, we wish you a Happy New Year, and pray that you are not only inscribed in The Book of Life…but more importantly, that you write your own chapters.

Regardless of your religious persuasion, Maddie's life journey reminds us of who is the author of our lives. Perhaps the scenery is not always in our control. Maybe the narrative turns in ways that are unimaginable. Yet no matter the circumstances, however extreme, no one can take away our voice as authors.

And if the time comes where we can no longer write for ourselves, may our cherished loved ones carry on our stories in our beautiful names.

I love you, Maddie. Your story will continue to shine light for many new years to come. L'Shana Tova.

Evening Reflections (9/9/18)

Team Maddie,

What a beautiful, powerful, and inspirational day. Today was a shining example of the far-reaching impact of Team Maddie. Pammy and I feel humbled, blessed, and proud both for Maddie and for such a special group of family, friends, and ever-growing team members.

At the same time, as Maddie's story hits home with new readers, my conversations today remind me that cancer has left all too many empty chairs in our lives. Yet even in those instances, we remain blessed and empowered to carry on our loved ones' stories.

In Maddie's case, let this post serve as a reminder that her Book of Life is not just a story in Maddie's honor. It's a story for anyone who has been touched by this devastating disease. A story for anyone with an empty chair at their table this year. A story for anyone with a hole in their heart. And a story for anyone moved by love, light, and inspiration.

Because of Team Maddie, every day, the Book of Life for me and Pammy is growing with more meaning. Each post adds a chapter. Every "like" drops a footnote. Each shared picture gives an illustration. In every which way, we are writing this next chapter together. And what a beautiful chapter it has been.

If there is one shining truth that today made clear it is as follows – this chapter is far from over. With over two-plus weeks of #ShineMaddiesLight to go, our collective story of inspiration will continue to bring light.

Keep Loving. Keep Writing. Keep Shining.

#ShineMaddiesLight: Day 10 of 30 (9/10/18)

Thank you, Maddie, for teaching me that sometimes the most important assistance we can offer someone on their journey is to just ensure they do not walk it alone.

Special thanks to the following local pediatric cancer organizations and their leaders/volunteers for walking Maddie's journey by our side: Anthony Rizzo Family Foundation; Andrew Weishar Foundation; Michael Matters Foundation; Bear Necessities; Make-A-Wish Illinois; Cancer Kiss My Cooley; and Flashes of Hope.

#ShineMaddiesLight: Day 11 of 30 (9/11/18)

Thank you, Maddie, for showing me how to find meaning in even the most unexpected places.

During Maddie's journey, we drew meaning everywhere from song quotes, to Daniel Tiger episodes, to Moana, to everyday coincidences. Meaning and inspiration were all around us. We just needed to be aware enough to receive their message.

Evening Reflections (9/11/18)

This morning's post centered around the importance of discovering meaning in the world around us. At no point in my life have I been more present than when standing by Maddie's side. That presence brought the gift of mindfulness. And from mindfulness spread meaning.

That meaning is beaming with unparalleled light, as Team Maddie continues to shine the lights of meaning, love, and inspiration on the world around us. As this march for meaning continues, Maddie's Miracles continue to grace my sights and sounds. After reflecting on the *Maddie's Miracles* chapter discussing the adventures and song lyrics of *Moana*, another animated song hit my iPhone today. A song by Maddie's other good buddy, Daniel Tiger, entitled *When Something Feels Bad, Turn it Around.*

While I'm probably the only person who choked up listening to this song today (or on any day for that matter), the message remains extraordinary in its simplicity. Daniel reminds us that no matter the struggle – whether simple or complex – the answer remains the same: choose light over dark. Love over hate. Joy over anger. A message that resonates so deeply on this September 11th day of remembrance. This day of light. This day of meaning.

#ShineMaddiesLight: Day 12 of 30 (9/12/18)

Thank you, Maddie, for teaching me that superheroes come in all sizes.

My superhero was 36.5 inches tall and 29.5 pounds of pure happiness. And she waged a war against cancer with her own personal Legion of Toon: Daniel Tiger, Peppa Pig, and Doc McStuffins. But even more importantly, she had seasoned Superheroes by her side. Special thanks to Anthony Rizzo, Abby Suarez, and the Anthony Rizzo Family Foundation for their incredible work in supporting families like ours fight this fight.

Evening Reflections (9/12/18)

Team Maddie,

What a beautiful day. I am filled with light, love, and inspiration at the shining show that our beautiful team put on today.

In honor of our Anthony Rizzo Family Foundation superheroes, the video clip included in this post from the ending scene of *The Natural* says all you need to know about today. Even if you're not a baseball fan, take a minute to watch the final home run scene in this baseball classic. It's well worth it. The spot-on symbolism on this day of sunlight is staggering.

No amount of pain keeps Team Maddie down. Instead, on the strength of the dynamic duo of Maddie and Anthony Rizzo, Team Maddie hit a home run of light that not even Roy Hobbs' light-inducing blast could match.

As we approach the halfway point of #ShineMaddiesLight, let's keep swinging for the fences. Post a message on Facebook. Write a book review on Amazon. Subscribe to our blog. Invite friends to follow the journey. Retweet our tweets. Post on Instagram. Buy a book for a friend. Or two. Or three. Keep talking. Keep sharing. Keep shining.

Thanks to you, this mammoth display of awareness is an awe-inspiring grand slam. We are making a difference. We are shining Maddie's light. We are #TeamMaddie.

#ShineMaddiesLight: Day 13 of 30 (9/13/18)

Thank you, Maddie, for teaching me that there is nothing more resilient than the human spirit…except the innocence and adaptability of a toddler.

Special thanks to Shirley Ryan AbilityLab for being the spirit behind so many resilient spirits.

Special Message: Unite to Shine Light (9/13/18)

Team Maddie,

This morning's post reflected on what was the absolute peak of Maddie's initial physical recovery from emergency surgery. More than one year ago, her return to Shirley Ryan put us face to face with how far we'd come. And yet those very same moments continue to inspire us today. They remain a shining example of Maddie's journey from paralysis to miraculous.

As with so many of Maddie's Miracles, even the precise words from today's chapter excerpt, as originally written, ring as true as ever:

At this moment, I am filled with pride for Maddie. For Pammy. For our parents. Siblings. Friends. Teachers. Classmates. Colleagues. And every one of you that has played a part in bringing joy to Maddie's life during this otherwise daunting time.

One year later, I am filled with the same sense of pride. For Maddie. For Team Maddie. For Light. For Love. For Life. In many ways, it's the pride of accomplishing what we have collectively been accomplishing since April 21st – keeping Maddie as

Maddie. And shining a bright, beautiful light on the world in the process.

With Maddie lighting the way, we now approach another peak in this journey. In two days – on September 15th – we reach the halfway point in our #ShineMaddiesLight campaign. We do so at a time when Team Maddie has never shined brighter.

With our roster at full strength, we're now going to dial up the electricity one more notch. To make the turning point of September a day of inspirational awareness to remember. A day where we will *Unite to Shine Light.*

On September 15th, we invite each and every one of our Team Maddie faithful to join in a powerful, united showing of awareness. To do so, please post a picture of yourself (or your family) with a copy of *Maddie's Miracles* in your hand. Share your favorite inspirational message, even if you've shared it before. And include two powerful hashtags:

#ShineMaddiesLight
#WeAreAware

After all, at its core, #ShineMaddiesLight is about awareness. When we announced our movement to #ShineMaddiesLight, the mission was best summed up as follows:

Our hope is that through our collective electricity, we are going to light up the social media world with one of the brightest lights ever seen. And that when Maddie's bright light is beaming through our shared messages of love and gratitude, the darkness of cancer will be but a blip on the radar. Instead, we'll raise awareness for the strength, the heroism, the inspiration, and the love that carries the families who have to move through this immovable disease. To remind us all why our work here is not done. That the other

Maddies of the world, and the other Kramers of the world, need our help. Not just because of the darkness of cancer. But because of the brightness of their light.

Together, with the incredible light and love of Team Maddie, we are showing the world exactly that. On September 15th, we'll unite in our powerful message. And build momentum toward the second half of this month of awareness and light.

Shine On, Team Maddie. Looking forward to seeing your shining faces online in two days!

#ShineMaddiesLight: Day 14 of 30 (9/14/18)

Thank you, Maddie, for teaching me the true mark of reaching the other side of the emotional mountain that is trauma: learning to live side by side with sadness as opposed to being subsumed by sadness.

Evening Reflections (9/14/18)

Team Maddie,

A friend and former colleague had some poignant thoughts about today's post:

"You know, in many ways this is the most special time in our lives." This is the definition of love and grace. This is why Maddie's Miracles is a book of life, not a book of despair. To any person struggling, or who has ever struggled, with an "asterisk" hovering overhead, I can't recommend this enough.

The asterisk in our lives. We all have them. It's just a matter of degree and character. If there's a definitive lesson Maddie left all of us, when it comes to life's asterisk, it is this:

Let It Go.

We keep moving. Asterisk and all. And tomorrow, we will all shine our collective asterisk. If you participate in one #ShineMaddiesLight post this year, make it this one. Tomorrow, in a united day of awareness, post a picture of you/your family holding a copy of *Maddie's Miracles*. Share your most touching takeaway from Maddie. And include two simple hashtags:

#ShineMaddiesLight
#WeAreAware

#ShineMaddiesLight: Day 15 of 30 (9/15/18)

Thank you, Maddie, for teaching me the transformative power of being aware.

Today's inspirational lesson reminds us that only from awareness can real change form. In honor of the thousands of lives touched by childhood cancer every year, and in honor of the blinding light that our heroes bring to their battles with the darkest of diseases, join us today as we Unite to Shine Light.

Evening Reflections (9/15/18)

Team Maddie,

Unite to Shine Light…did we ever.

Scanning through the beautiful posts upon posts tonight, we are reminded of the beauty of inspiration. The beauty of community. The beauty of light.

We are also reminded of the beauty of the many miracles that Maddie has blessed us with. Disease does not just mean darkness. Cancer does not just mean conclusion. One of the most incredible miracles of light is this: light reflects. Light grows brighter and broader with every mirror that aids its beautiful glow. Light Begets Light.

Today, our bright and beautiful Team Maddie showed the world that darkness will never defeat light. And the impact of that light show is incredible. With every post, every picture, every retweet, every repost…Team Maddie is reaching new people. Team Maddie is bringing people together. Team Maddie is uniting old friends. Team Maddie is connecting new friends. Team Maddie is shining light.

As we move toward the second and strongest half of #ShineMaddieLight, I want to share one shining example of our connectivity and electricity. A few days ago, a person who I didn't know commented on the Facebook timeline of an old high school friend who now lives in Texas. The commenter posted a special note about Maddie's story, so I reached out directly to thank her. A few days later, I put together that she works for the Wood Family Foundation. A few days after that, I remember that the Wood Family Foundation is responsible for the place that brought us the single most amount of light in the face of our darkness:

The 17th Floor Playroom at Lurie's Place.

Yes, all because of #ShineMaddiesLight, and the collective shining of our powerful Team Maddie, the team behind our biggest source of light has now joined our light-filled movement. Thank you, Laura Muriello and the Wood Family Foundation, for your efforts to bring light where there would otherwise be darkness. Thank you for helping to #ShineMaddiesLight. And thank you for being a shining example of philanthropy and community.

#ShineMaddiesLight: Day 16 of 30 (9/16/18)

Thank you, Maddie, for teaching me that the title to the First Dance song from Mommy and Daddy's wedding is timeless. In sickness and in health, these words will always ring true: Don't Stop Believin'.

Evening Reflections (9/16/18)

"With Maddie by our side (or more accurately, with Maddie leading the way with unparalleled strength), we will not stop believing. We will not fade to black. We will hold on to that feeling." (Excerpt from *Maddie's Miracles* chapter entitled "Don't Stop Believin'").

As we move into the final two weeks of #ShineMaddiesLight, this is our fight song. We will not stop believing. We will not fade to black. We will hold on to that feeling.

The belief, the color, the shining feeling that is #ShineMaddiesLight is best seen tonight in the post of Danielle (re-printed below). Danielle is a Pediatric Oncology Nurse at the University of Iowa. We never met before #ShineMaddiesLight began. Yet everything from the beautiful color in her backdrop, to the brightness of her smile, to the inspiration of her life's work, is the essence of #ShineMaddiesLight. Bear in mind that Danielle works directly with the very same patients afflicted by this otherwise dark disease. And there's a reason she can proudly stand tonight, in all of her color and brightness, and shout their inspiration to the world. The same reason we #ShineMaddiesLight. The same reason we are #TeamMaddie. The same reason #WeAreAware.

Keep Shining, Danielle. Keep Shining, Team Maddie. And keep adding so much beautiful color to our timelines and this special time in our lives. As post by post, and photo by photo, we continue to add color and brightness to the pediatric cancer world.

<u>Danielle's Post</u>

Since yesterday, September 15th, was the halfway point for Pediatric Cancer Awareness Month & the #ShineMaddiesLight campaign, I am sharing a picture of myself with my copy of *Maddie's Miracles* at one of the places that means the world to me & is the same place I met Maddie's incredible Aunt Jamie Kramer.

For the last two years, I have been blessed to take care of the bravest kids I have ever met. I would like to thank all of them and Maddie for helping me become the nurse & person I am today! Thank you for your hope, your joy, your love, your happiness & sunshine! We've shared some of the best times together at end of chemo and bone marrow transplant parties, playing & doing crafts, and everything in between…and some of the worst moments that no child & family should ever have to experience. Your resilience and strength has taught me to never take anything for granted, to never stress the small stuff, to be kind every chance I get and that life is so so precious!

I feel so lucky to be a Pediatric Oncology Nurse & even luckier to care for the strongest children in the world!

#ShineMaddiesLight: Day 17 of 30 (9/17/18)

Thank you, Lily (we didn't forget about you, Lily Bug!), for teaching me that the brightest flowers only grow more colorful from the storm.

Evening Reflections (9/17/18)

Team Maddie,

Lily was so excited about all of the Team Maddie love today. Still trying to shed her newborn reputation reflected in today's post, Lily is in the process of forming the #LilyBugClub as we speak. Luckily, she hasn't learned how to use Instagram or Facebook yet, so we have a little more time.

The only experiences that rivaled Lily's joy of Team Maddie's bright light today were the sights and sounds of the dolphins she witnessed at Shedd Aquarium this afternoon. Watching her in action places me front and center with what makes children so incredible. Their inherent senses of joy, wonder, and love remain a constant source of inspiration.

While we strive to impart so much knowledge upon our children, Maddie and Lily remind me that if we could only just master the knowledge that they already harbor at such a young age, how much better off we all would be. There is a reason each and every post this month begins with the simple words: Thank you, Maddie/Lily, for teaching me...

Because as much as we worked tirelessly to show Maddie and Lily the path forward, they were always the ones leading the way. And they continue to do so today, as we continue to reflect the bright light that they shine upon us.

Keep Shining, Team Maddie. And remember that as we shine, we do so on behalf of those who provide us so much vibrant light.

#ShineMaddiesLight: Day 18 of 30 (9/18/18)

Thank you, Maddie, for teaching me the importance of coming back to one simple question in order to stay focused in the face of adversity: What's next?

Evening Reflections (9/18/18)

What's next?

What's immediately next?

What's immediately next is that Pammy and I are going to take a moment to bask in the beautiful light that Team Maddie has shined in every direction today. We are eighteen days into this beautiful month of awareness. With no sign of slowing down, Team Maddie filled our timelines with messages of love, life, and inspiration.

Team Maddie's impact is going beyond our social media pages. By example, Team Maddie All-Star, Jami S., donated her hair today in honor of Maddie and Childhood Cancer Awareness Month. According to Jami (and apparently quoting my sister), "Because some fighter deserves this hair so much more."

Thank you, Jami, and thank you to all of Team Maddie for coming out in full force on this 18th day. A true day of life. Despite my focus on the present, I am confident that what's next is that we will continue to #ShineMaddiesLight in the most inspirational way imaginable.

#ShineMaddiesLight: Day 19 of 30 (9/19/18)

Thank you, Maddie, for teaching me that growth is not just measured in inches. For Maddie, her physical size was dwarfed by her miles and miles of spirit.

Evening Reflections (9/19/18)

Team Maddie,

Re-living Maddie's incredible ascension and growth during her treatment protocol remains about as inspirational as it gets. Her growing spirit. Her growing energy. Her growing light that she shined upon those blessed to watch her journey live or from afar.

Equally remarkable, the same is true for Team Maddie during this Childhood Cancer Awareness Month. Our growth is not just measured in books sold, money raised, or physical demarcations. It is instead in the light we are shining upon the world. The meaning we are adding into our lives and the lives of others. Our growth is exhibited any time a new member of Team Maddie shines light for the first time. Or when a long-term follower shares a special message that inspires his/her circle of friends. Or when a particular post prompts a moment of genuine reflection or charitable action.

These gifts of light. These gifts of life. These gifts of humanity. These are the collective gifts that Maddie's growth left all of us...and they are the very same gifts that Team Maddie is now providing the world around us with each light of awareness that we shine.

In honor of this beautiful legacy of light, feel free to share this morning's entry with someone new. And continue our growth in a way that defies inches…

#ShineMaddiesLight: Day 20 of 30 (9/20/18)

Thank you, Maddie, for teaching me two critical words for conquering the chaos that is cancer (or any life challenge with an uncertain outcome): We'll See.

Evening Reflections (9/20/18)

Today's inspirational post touched upon the importance of "we'll see." The power of embracing the unknown. Accepting that certain parts of our lives are out of our control. Although this psychological surrender supported Maddie's serenity, it was not at the expense of her security. After all, even with this pocket of uncertainty, or her love for "soup and two surprises," there was always one driving force of consistency and security:

Mommy.

While I may be the voice of Maddie's stories, Pammy was the heart and soul behind Maddie's ascension. The smiles upon smiles that you see in Maddie were a direct reflection of Pammy's unending love. Despite living and breathing the unimaginable day in and day out. Despite the universe lining up reason after reason to get knocked down. Or worse yet, reason after reason to stay down. Obstacle after obstacle, challenge after challenge, one of the main aspects of Maddie's life that was never subject to "we'll see" was the love, support, and smiles of her Mommy.

Thank you, Pammy, for teaching me what it really means to be a warrior mom. And to fight for your children with the unparalleled weapon of love.

#ShineMaddiesLight: Day 21 of 30 (9/21/18)

Thank you, Maddie, for teaching me that enduring hardship requires a consistent narrative framework. Our family's recipe? The truth. Broken down. With a personalized dash of fun.

Special thanks to the unsung heroes of the cancer battle: the child life specialists. Our narrative, and therefore Maddie's trusting, secure, and joy-filled journey through darkness would not have been the same without you. You taught us how to write a narrative. You gave us the vocabulary. You set our scene. You provided us sample screenplays. You are an absolute gift to the medical community. And the lessons you left us not only helped write Maddie's story, but they continue to guide us as we move forward today.

Evening Reflections (9/21/18)

Team Maddie,

A few weeks ago, the American Cancer Society approached me and Pammy with a concept to assist other families who are caring for a child with cancer. They asked us to create a variety of homemade selfie videos where we would answer a number of questions about certain aspects of the journey. At the time, we had no idea how the selfie video would be used, which questions/answers they would address, or any other detail.

Fast forward to today. This morning, Pammy and I posted our daily #ShineMaddiesLight post. The topic for Day 21 centered around the importance of The Narrative and honest, truthful communication with your child (with, of course, a dash of fun). Well, by pure coincidence, on this very same day, the American Cancer Society published the work product they had been planning with our various selfie videos. And of all footage, of all the questions/answers, what topic did they portray?

The Narrative.

It is a privilege to be able to share our experience with other parents enduring the unimaginable. And we hope that this simple but critical message will help guide their journeys. The video reminds me that Maddie's bright light is shining not just rays of inspiration but also those of education and guidance. Special thanks to the American Cancer Society for their ongoing efforts to educate, raise awareness, and attack cancer from every angle.

Keep shining, Maddie. We love you. And we pray that through our continued efforts, we will continue to leave this dark cancer world a brighter place than when it met us.

#ShineMaddiesLight: Day 22 of 30 (9/22/18)

Thank you, Maddie, for teaching me the joy of memorializing each mile marker on the marathon that is life.

Evening Reflections (9/22/18)

Team Maddie,

As Pammy and I know all too well, milestones come and go. But we all have the ability to recognize those moments when they arrive. To embrace them instead of just letting them pass. And to hold on and memorialize in a manner that does them justice to create memories that will last a lifetime.

Team Maddie is living one of those moments right now. These past three weeks of #ShineMaddiesLight have been nothing short of miraculous. Thanks to your incredible generosity both on and off social media, we are inspiring new people each and every day.

As these final eight days of September arrive, let's embrace this moment. Make your mark on #ShineMaddiesLight. Don't let the days pass you by. Post a photo on Facebook or Instagram of your favorite passage. Write a review on Amazon. Share a post of another Team Maddie member that inspires you. Subscribe to our blog. E-mail friends, family, colleagues, or other contacts to join our journey of inspiration. Whatever your ray of choice, just keep shining.

And in the end, we all just might have more memories that will last a lifetime.

#ShineMaddiesLight: Day 23 of 30 (9/23/18)

Thank you, Maddie, for teaching me that, in the musical of life, every once in awhile we all just need a restful moment to be nothing more than a member of the audience...in someone else's show.

Special thanks to Bear Necessities, a local nonprofit organization, for gifting us a memory of experiencing life in the audience that will stay with us for the rest of our lives. Your "Bear Hug" program – which offers customized experiences for cancer patients and families – is a blessing to all of those who feel your charitable embrace.

Evening Reflections (9/23/18)

This morning's post, and the excerpt from the *Maddie's Miracles* chapter entitled "The Audience," not only details one of the more welcome reprieves during Maddie's journey, but it also highlights another underlying theme...

The importance of music.

Throughout Maddie's life – including during her battle with cancer – music, dancing, and art were truly the beautiful stuff of which life was made. The moments where meaning shined the brightest. Even just a quick skimming of the chapter titles of *Maddie's Miracles* conveys how important music has been as a guide and a source of fulfillment. Oftentimes, life is art and art is life. We feel that more than ever as we continue to rise above the unimaginable.

Thank you, Team Maddie, for helping us continue to write these special verses of Maddie's inspirational song. Your posts, your likes, your shares, your Amazon reviews, your smiles, your tears, your offline conversations, and your private messages of love and support all continue to create this beautiful melody. A melody that I know has a certain little girl shimmy shaking with pride as the world sings in her honor.

#ShineMaddiesLight: Day 24 of 30 (9/24/18)

Thank you, Maddie, for teaching me the importance of maintaining an attitude of gratitude. Or as I now call it, Maddie-tude.

Special thanks to all of Team Maddie for your unwavering support for Maddie and our family. To say that enduring medical hardship "takes a village" would be an understatement. We have been blessed with an entire country's worth of support (both literally and figuratively). Family support, friend support, colleague support, employer support, philanthropic support, medical support, nursing care support, and community support.

You are all the collective reason we had the strength to give our very best to Maddie. And with your continued support, I have no doubt that we'll continue to shine Maddie's light upon this world both during and after Childhood Cancer Awareness Month. To ensure that other families enduring this battle always at least have one extra beam of light shining down upon them.

Evening Reflections (9/24/18)

A Day of Gratitude. A Day of Team Maddie.

These two concepts are forever intertwined in my heart. Thank you all for continuing to inspire our writing, our actions, and our lives. Tonight, I share the post of Team Maddie member, Kim. Kim's photo (of a memorial wall at her workplace) encapsulates our movement of light. And reminds us that Maddie's presence, and her light-filled messages, are often visible in our daily lives. The places we pass every day. The sounds we hear on a regular basis. If we just keep our eyes open, the light always seems to make its way in...

The memorial wall reads as follows: "Rather than mourn the absence of the flame, let us celebrate how brightly it burned."

#ShineMaddiesLight: Day 25 of 30 (9/25/18)

Thank you, Maddie, for teaching me that, in times of joy and in sorrow, we are all better when we're dancing.

Evening Reflections (9/25/18)

Better when we're dancing.

What a powerful concept. If anyone new to Team Maddie had any questions as to the power of Maddie's inspirational moves, one glance at the video from today's post (available on our original blog post dated September 25, 2018) would be proof enough.

It wasn't just Maddie's legs that danced…her personality danced. Every single inch of her body oozed with a dancing aura. I watch her in action, and it's like watching a being from another world. Her energy. Her spirit. Her smile. Showing us time and time again – light shines brighter than any darkness can overshadow.

Team Maddie's social media dance is proving equally bright. What a beautiful performance today. With just five days left in #ShineMaddiesLight, let's save our best moves for last. For those new to Team Maddie, there are three special steps to this dance:

Step One: post an inspirational message or passage from *Maddie's Miracles*.

Step Two: share a post from a fellow Team Maddie member that moves you.

Step Three: write a review on Amazon to preview our dance for others.

Keep dancing, Team Maddie. And the world will continue to be a brighter place.

#ShineMaddiesLight: Day 26 of 30 (9/26/18)

Thank you, Lily, for teaching me that sometimes before you move forward you must move backward.

Evening Reflections (9/26/18)

"I know that forward will come eventually. No matter what. Fueled by the same Miracles and Lights that powered this otherwise blessed year." (*Maddie's Miracles*, A New Year's Lesson from Lily).

Fitting that today, of all days, was a day of forward. A day of looking ahead to the future. Of the hope in the distance. As we moved forward on Day 26 of #ShineMaddiesLight, Pammy and I had the opportunity to speak at two special events.

This morning, I sat on a panel for a local high school assembly. The discussion topic centered around finding a source of inspiration from which to effectuate change. I couldn't possibly envision a conversation more forward-thinking than this inspired talk with 150 motivated students.

Eleven hours later, we were invited to join a small Lurie Children's gathering of young professionals committed to funding a group-selected research project for pediatric cancer care. Our role was to share Maddie's story and continue to add a personal touch to their efforts to move research and medical progress forward.

A day of forward. Motivated by two special little girls. As Lily would remind us…

Go Go Go!

#ShineMaddiesLight: Day 27 of 30 (9/27/18)

Thank you, Maddie, for teaching me to be able to see the bright light of inspiration through the clouds of sadness.

Evening Reflections (9/27/18)

The video from this morning's post (available on our blog post dated September 27, 2018) is a particularly powerful clip to re-experience. Maddie's running, frog leaping, hide n' seeking, and snailing awesomeness was filmed on December 23, 2017. Eight months after her April paralysis. Twelve days before January 4th.

I very much feel that yin and yang in this video. Here she was, in the peak of her recovery. Showing us all, in true Maddie form, how far she had come. And how she could light up a room even in the darkest of hours. And yet at the same time, as one of the last videos of Maddie filmed in our home, it's a poignant reminder of the fragility of life.

But one feeling that is not (and will never be) fragile is our commitment to #ShineMaddiesLight. With just three days left, let's give every ounce of inspiration we have. For Maddie. For Cancer Awareness. For every family who has ever had to, or will ever have to, walk this walk.

#ShineMaddiesLight: Day 28 of 30 (9/28/18)

Thank you, Maddie, for teaching me the power of a promise.

Special thanks to the Ann & Robert H. Lurie Children's Hospital of Chicago (or, as Maddie called it, "Lurie's Place") for working tirelessly to fulfill your promise to our family and other patients across the country in need of your care. We promise to always be by your side.

Evening Reflections (9/28/18)

Today's #ShineMaddiesLight post centered around the power of promise. With just two more days remaining in Childhood Cancer Awareness Month, Pammy and I extend this promise to Team Maddie:

We are not done shining.

Yes, the calendar's version of Childhood Cancer Awareness Month concludes on September 30th. But we are committed to ensuring that Maddie's light will continue to shine well beyond the end of this month.

The back cover of *Maddie's Miracles* refers to Maddie as providing "the gift of this beautiful book of life." Our hope is that *Maddie's Miracles* remains a source of life, a source of light, and a source of inspiration and change for years to come. And thus as we move beyond Childhood Cancer Awareness Month, our vision is to continue to use 100% of the net proceeds that we receive from *Maddie's Miracles* toward efforts that #ShineMaddiesLight. Efforts of awareness. Efforts of community impact. Efforts of charity. Efforts of change. Efforts of inspiration. Maddie provided us this beautiful gift of life and so we too shall continue to give that same gift of life to the world in her beautiful honor.

Without question, our ability to #ShineMaddiesLight is only as strong as our incredible Team Maddie. We have made an indelible mark of love and light this month and that is all due to your bright, beautiful souls. So keep shining, dear friends. Keep carrying Maddie's messages and stories in your heart. Keep spreading the word about *Maddie's Miracles*. Keep sharing the gifts of life performed in her honor. And keep up your inspiring efforts to #ShineMaddiesLight.

#ShineMaddiesLight: Day 29 of 30 (9/29/18)

Thank you, Maddie, for teaching me that there are no stronger weapons in any war than love and inspiration.

Special thanks to the American Cancer Society for all you do to fight the war against cancer. Pammy and I will always ensure that you never have to fight alone.

Evening Reflections (9/29/18)

Love and inspiration.

You have all given us those two feelings in spades this past month. Thank you for helping to #ShineMaddiesLight. Thank you for sharing #MaddiesMiracles. Thank you for being #TeamMaddie.

For those who haven't watched this morning's video before, please take a moment to view the YouTube clip in today's blog post. The filmed speech remains a special tribute to Maddie and the surrounding army that it takes to engage in a battle with cancer.

As I proclaimed during our emotional remarks, "although Maddie's battle with cancer might be over, her war – and our war – is just beginning."

As our war continues, let's give these last 24 hours of Childhood Cancer Awareness Month every ounce of love, life, and light in our bodies. Leave your mark. Light your light. Write your review on Amazon. Buy copies of *Maddie's Miracles* for friends, family, or those in need of inspiration. Share Maddie's story in a way that leads to prolonged light. And most importantly, continue to keep her in your inspired and loving heart as you move forward in your life's journey.

#ShineMaddiesLight: Day 30 of 30 (9/30/18)

Thank you, Maddie, for teaching me that a complete life's story has no endings. Only new beginnings. And as this Childhood Cancer Awareness Month reaches Day 30, it is with endless love, passion, and meaning that we share with you the latest new beginning to our Book of Life. We welcome each and every one of you to help write this next special chapter, which can be found on the next page...

Prologue Revisited (9/30/18)

On September 30, 2018, Pammy and I added the words that follow as a new, next chapter to the ever-continuing story of Maddie's Miracles:

Team Maddie,

As the publication date for *Maddie's Miracles* grew near, committing to a final chapter became increasingly difficult. To be honest, I struggled with including any ending to Maddie's story. Feeling as if her story should not conclude in any way, shape, or form. Because my prayer is that there is no conclusion to Maddie. That Maddie, her life, and her legacy shall instead transform into one giant love-filled ellipsis, which will dance on for eternity.

Although I attempted to ease the emotional burden by referring to the last chapter as "The New Beginning," the final chapter nonetheless memorialized the words I relayed at Maddie's funeral on January 7, 2018. But Maddie's story did not end on January 7th. Nor shall her beautiful Book of Life. Today, in honor of the ellipsis that will be Maddie's eternal literary light, we share this Prologue Revisited with endless love and appreciation.

For those who have been following our blog since April 2017, or for those who are reading Maddie's story for the first time, the conclusion to Maddie's physical time here on this Earth came quickly. The unexpected, rapid conclusion to this Book of Life mirrored our all-too-rapid reality. But equally rapid was our commitment to ensure that Maddie's legacy was that of inspiration. To honor our promise to move forward with a dance in our step and a smile on our face.

And so this Prologue Revisited is very much a true new beginning. Because on this September 30, 2018, we announce the formation of our new lifelong, philanthropic commitment:

Dancing While Cancering
The Maddie Kramer Foundation

Formed in Maddie's honor, our 501(c)(3) nonprofit organization has one loving mission:

Bringing joy to the inpatient hospital experience for children with cancer.

As promised, Pammy, Lily, and I are going to channel Maddie in the same ways that she inspired the world. In doing so, we are dedicated to helping existing and future patients battle cancer just as Maddie battled hers. Through dancing. Through singing. Through imagination. Through character playing. And through all the unbridled positivity that Maddie brought to her energetic, playful, and inspirational waltz across life's stage.

With the powers of love, life, and light, there are no endings. Only new beginnings. Thank you to Team Maddie, for continuing to give us the strength to keep going. And thank you to Maddie, our one in a million hero, for inspiring each and every step of our life's dance.

We love you, sweet girl…

Evening Reflections (9/30/18)

"Once we take our moments to mourn, Pammy, Lily, and I are dedicated to ensuring that the Miracles and Lights that Maddie has bestowed upon all of us are spread well beyond our family and friend circle. That Maddie continues to make her mark on the world around her. And that when we all channel Maddie, we don't just channel tears. We instead channel dancing. We channel singing. We channel imagination. We channel character playing. We channel strength. We channel love. We channel life. I love you so much, Maddie. You will be with us wherever we go. Carrying us forward just as you always have. With a dance in our step, and a smile on our face." (*Maddie's Miracles*, Daddy's Eulogy).

With a dance in our step, and a smile on our face...

And with a full heart, Pammy and I want to thank each and every one of you for today's beautiful dance and endless smiles. Together, I know we will continue to create more dancing and more smiles...for children who need them more than ever.

Keep Dancing, Team Maddie. We love you.

#ShineMaddiesLight Update (10/1/18)

Team Maddie,

As Maddie's light begins shining into October, I am reminded of perhaps the most important lesson that Maddie gifted to us all:

You can't always choose the music life plays for you, but you can choose the way you dance to it.

For eight-and-a-half months, Maddie was Dancing While Cancering. And on the strength of those two dancing legs, once feared to never be able to walk again, she lifted the spirits of all of those blessed to join her journey.

Dancing While Cancering is not just an organization. It's a mindset. A dancing mindset that Maddie, at just three-and-a-half years old, gifted to her family and friends. A dancing mindset that we are dedicated to sharing with the world.

Pammy and I are blessed to have you joining this inspirational dance. Please help keep the dance going today with two beautiful hashtags and one beautiful link:

#DancingWhileCancering #ShineMaddiesLight

http://dancingwhilecancering.org

Team Maddie Forever,

Scott & Pammy

A Lifelong Prologue Revisited (1/1/20)

As you know by now, we don't do endings in the Kramer Family. We keep going. We keep beginning. We keep living. We keep surviving. And Maddie keeps shining.

24 months since Maddie's last sleepover at Lurie's Place, 24 months since the initial seeds of #ShineMaddiesLight and Dancing While Cancering were sprinkled, we have been blessed with a forest of inspiration and impact. Filled with the bold and beautiful trees of life, light, and love, Dancing While Cancering is officially partnered with 14 hospitals in 9 states as of today. Every newly diagnosed pediatric cancer patient at these incredible institutions is able to receive a "Smile Pack" courtesy of Dancing While Cancering. Courtesy of Maddie's inspiration. Inside this bright backpack, heroic pediatric cancer patients across the country will find numerous, fun-filled goodies to help further brighten their hospital stays. Room decorations. Musical instruments. A wireless speaker. All beautiful rays of the bright light that Maddie shined on the world. Each backpack delivered standing as a physical representation of the love, light, and meaning packed into Maddie's full and miraculous life.

To this day, I do not spend time focusing on how Maddie could have possibly left this physical world so soon.

Or on how a loving god could take such a beautiful angel from our physical presence. In the famous words of Nietzsche, which were reinforced in Victor Frankl's *Man's Search for Meaning*, "He who has a Why to live for can bear almost any How." As with our original Book of Life, we are writing our own Why. We are finding meaning in every step of our life's journey. We are making a conscious commitment to continue to carry Maddie's meaning with us along that journey. To continue to shine her beautiful light until our own lights dim. And when that time comes, may the miracles that follow continue to honor us with the most inspirational blessing that anyone may be bestowed. The ultimate symbol of a life of meaning:

That another will be inspired to continue to carry the torch holding our hopefully eternal flame of hope…

Made in the USA
Monee, IL
04 January 2020